Streets Paved with Hope

A Bitter Sweet Search for Love

Patrick Lee

www.streetspavedwithhope.com

Acknowledgements

I want to express my gratitude and thanks to the following:

The people of those streets in Donnybrook, Home Villas, Pembroke Cottages, Beaver Row and Beech Hill, whose kindness I will never forget.

Dublin Corporation for renting us a home for £1 per week.

Cecilia Molinari, our friend in New York, for her advice and help with the editing.

My three children, Gillian, Brian and Peter for opening up my life in ways I could never have thought possible. Especially Peter who provided invaluable support in bringing this book to print.

And finally, Pauline, my extraordinary wife, who's care, persistence and patience in helping me write this book, ensured that every word written expressed exactly what I wanted to say. This was a labour of love for her and I am eternally grateful for this love.

Contents

Prologue

One night, as I lay in bed, drifting in and out of sleep, I had a clear vision of myself walking down a long, winding road that was familiar to me. The only light was that of the moon, trapped in a soft mist. And there he stood, in short trousers held up with braces, where I had left him. It was me as a young boy, cowering in terror, with tears rolling down my face. I saw myself embrace him, and then as I walked on, I slowly reclaimed my damaged and lost eight-, ten-, seventeen-, twenty-one-, and twenty-four-year-old selves. The enormity and significance of my experiences as a boy and young man suddenly became clear and, as we merged, I felt a sense of oneness, my spirit rejuvenated. I was finally whole again.

Chapter 1

Home Villas

I was born in Dublin in the spring of 1949, quickly followed by my twin sister, Philomena. We now had five children in our family, a magic number when it came to entitlement to rent, for one pound a week, a government-sponsored corporation house. Our new home was a "two-up, two-down" at 25 Home Villas in the south side neighbourhood of Donnybrook. Here a small group of corporation houses were placed between some beautiful, privately owned residences and the lush greenery of Herbert Park. From the top of the road, our house was camouflaged within a row of identical small, two-story, redbrick, terraced houses with wood-framed windows.

The first clear memory I have of 25 Home Villas was a grey, wet afternoon rattled by a horrendous thunder and lightning storm. I was five years old, but can still remember the rain pounding the pavement, the bright streaks of lightning filling the sky, and the sound of thunder bellowing in my ears. I was with my Ma, brothers and sisters, and we were all clustered around the narrow front room window frightened yet mesmerised by what was happening. As we stared into an overcast sky illuminated by bolts of light, we spotted the fruit and vegetable cart struggling down the street and parking outside our house. The owner, Christy, was a formidable, intimidating sight. He wore wellington boots, a heavy overcoat gathered in at the waist by a huge leather belt, and an oilcloth pulled up over his head covering his peaky hat. The poor horse that pulled the cart held his head low and was soaked by the rain beating down his back - a sorry sight.

Suddenly, Ma swung the front door open and invited Christy in to shelter from the storm. Then, to our surprise, we heard her say to him, "Should we bring the poor horse in, he's terrified?" As Christy stepped inside, he replied with a slight smirk on his face, "No, Mam, he'll be fine." I felt sorry for the animal, but also breathed a sigh of relief, unable to imagine how this horse would get through the door let alone fit in our small front room. The storm eventually passed, Christy went on his way, and all returned to normal. Never in my wildest dreams could I have imagined then what a crucial role this man, his horse, and his cart would play in my life.

Twenty-five Home Villas was also where my uncle Michael, Da's brother, used to visit us occasionally. He was a "confirmed bachelor", bald like our father, with a sneering, jeering way about him and even though we were already tight for space, we had to accommodate him. At the end of one visit, he handed Ma a gift of five Irish Sweepstake tickets, saying "Thanks for looking after me." She quickly put them in her apron pocket with a hint of a smile on her lips. Next thing Uncle Michael added, " Of course, if you win anything, I expect you to share fifty-fifty with me." Ma's cheeks reddened with fury as she whipped the tickets out of her apron pocket and threw them back at him. " Stick them up your arse," she said, "you're not welcome here." Harsh words, spoken with such a fierce look in her eyes that he was left in no doubt, and neither was I, that Ma was not a woman to be trifled with. He never stayed with us again.

About a year later, we moved across the street from 25 to 6 Home Villas, the place I would call home well into my early twenties. This house was on the sunny side of the street and had a south-facing garden overlooking the park. Ma got wind that the tenants were planning to move to a private house and set about securing this superior location before their move became common knowledge. She reached out to Dr French O'Carroll, the local medical officer, who championed our cause with the housing authorities. The request was approved on the basis that my eldest

11

sister, Joan, who suffered from asthma, would benefit greatly from the cleaner air across the street. And so, under the dim light of the street lamps, over we trundled back and forth, carrying everything we owned into our new home—dismantled beds, furniture, kitchenware, and clothes. Ma refused to move earlier in the day, even though we had the keys that afternoon because she didn't want anyone to see our meagre possessions. I had never before been on the street after 6:00 p.m., so the quietness and darkness heightened the excitement of the whole event.

On the first morning in our new home, we stood downstairs, taking in our new surroundings. The house itself was identical to the one we came from: a skylight framed the top of the stairs and the entrances to two bedrooms and a cubby hole built into the eves. On the ground floor, there was another cubby hole under the stairs for coats, boots, bags, and all sorts of bits. Here also were two small rooms with fireplaces, and a scullery with a sink and cooker, leading to an outside toilet and coal shed. The one big difference between this and our previous home was the back garden. At number 25, we had a tiny, dark yard whereas our new garden was magnificent. It got the sun all day, was thirty-six-foot-long, surrounded by high redbrick walls, and just beyond this, the crowning glory: Herbert Park. We couldn't believe our luck, my siblings and I could hardly contain our joy and Ma was in her element. She had just pulled off a major coup, we now had the biggest sunny garden, on the street. Here she could have a long clothesline and plenty of space to plant her rhubarb and ferns, reminders of her proud country origins.

Ma was from Cloghore in County Donegal, a stone's throw from the famous Belleek Pottery factory across the border in Northern Ireland. The eldest girl of eight children, Ma led a simple country life before moving to Dublin as a teenager. Here she could make a living for herself and send money home to help support the rest of her family. In Dublin, she worked for Sir Joseph Glynn, a well-to-do respected politician, in the kitchen of his house on Ailesbury Road. This position, she felt elevated her country-girl status, and when she later married and had children, she took great pride in bragging about her job. She even went to great lengths to emulate some of the housing décors she had seen in this grand residence, eventually fitting our front room with an unsuitable chaise longue. This was also probably where she developed her cookery skills. Even though sparsely rationed, my mouth still waters with the thought of her roast potatoes, steamed puddings, trifles and apple tarts.

When Ma baked, she would sit the younger children, Philomena, myself and our younger brother Michael, around the table. She promised us that if we sat quietly and behaved, she'd make us some tartlets with the leftover pastry, something well worth waiting on. Ma was a small, rotund, woman, who wore slippers, an apron, a knitted hat and a shawl around her shoulders in the house, even when baking. We watched her in awe and with great anticipation as she went through the whole process: cleaning down the formica tabletop; mixing the ingredients; lightly kneading the ball of pastry and rolling it out on the table which had been sprinkled generously with fistfuls of flour to prevent it sticking. She then placed a layer of pastry on the baking tray, piled in slices of apples, gooseberries, or rhubarb and loads of sugar, and carefully laid more pastry on top. Finally, the edges were trimmed and sealed by pressing with her thumb or a fork, egg yolk brushed on top, and holes pierced to allow the steam to escape while cooking.

Our tartlets were then prepared from the pastry cuttings, filled with strawberry jam, and cooked alongside the tart. We were transfixed as we watched Ma cautiously open the oven door now and again to check on progress. A delightful aroma wafted around the room, teasing us with anticipation. When cooked, the tart was put away for Sunday dessert or visitors, but our little jam rolls with their beautiful brown crusts and jam seeping from each end were all we wanted and eventually, we got our reward.

Another treat was the delicious hot buttered toast we had on cold dark winter afternoons. This was before we had a TV in the backroom and we used to sit there in front of the open fire.

Ma would let us make our own toast by holding a slice of bread on a fork in front of the flames. Because our little fingers were easily burned, we used to put socks on our hands as the bread slowly turned brown. Ma would then coat each slice with golden butter. This toast making and the whole baking experience are some of the few fond memories I still have of life with Ma. As the three of us younger children got older and less docile, our role as her little angels quickly dissipated, to our detriment. She became distant, indifferent and at times very cruel to me. But this didn't stop me trying to be close to her, it just made me more needy and desperate, to please.

Ma suffered a lot from shingles, just above her knee, and used to scratch them fiercely until they bled. I hated to see her in pain, but there was nothing I could do for her. Because she was overweight, she had great difficulty washing her feet. When she asked me to help, I never hesitated, although it wasn't something I relished. I hoped this would bring us closer together and longed for her to show she cared. I waited for her to wrap her arms around me and kiss me, but she never did.

She seldom went out unless to go shopping, take the train home to Donegal, or to bring us to Herbert Park, a rare event. She never really settled or felt comfortable in the city and believed her country origins set her apart from the "Jackeens" (a derogatory term for someone from Dublin). As far as she was concerned "they were not our kind". While we were born in Dublin, we were raised as if we were "Culchies" (country folk) and were adamantly discouraged from mixing with our neighbours. All of this inevitably alienated us and deprived us of participating in what was a very sociable community.

My Da also chose to keep our neighbours at arm's length and unfortunately did the same with us children. I don't ever remember him speaking to me directly unless to chastise or ask me to get something for him. But, I do remember that, from an early age, he had no interest in me and his disdainful glances when I tried to engage with him made this clear to me. One day, when I was about six, he confronted me unexpectedly. I had left the whites of the egg on my plate, which was usual for me because I hated them. Next thing Da came and stood over me menacingly, insisted I eat them and forced them down my throat. I started to dry wretch and cried bitterly. I was trembling, feeling brutalised, but he just carried on as if nothing had happened. That was the last day egg whites ever passed my lips.

Da was from Thomastown, County Kilkenny, where his family had a shop and ran a taxi service. I would have loved to know more about their business interests and my aunts and uncles, on the Lee side, but he never spoke to us about them, or his upbringing. All I know is that he left home in his teens to join the army in Dublin and acquired a reputation as a good boxer. He was a big, strong, good-looking man, with a moustache and bald head, and was meticulous about his appearance. His suits, jackets, and trousers were always pressed, and his shoes shined. As a child, I wanted so much to be like him, smartly dressed from head to toe.

I used to watch him through the kitchen window as he went about the ritual of polishing his shoes in the back garden. I was fascinated to see him take his bag of brushes, rags and polishes from the press under the kitchen sink and walk purposefully outside. He scooped the polish up with a rag and took great care to spread it into every crevice, one shoe at a time. The polish was left on for a few minutes, and then the vigorous brushing and shining began, inch by inch, until the shoes were gleaming. Holding them up to the sky, he would scrutinise each shoe with an air of satisfaction and pride. It was remarkable how much care and attention he gave to things that were important to him while his family's needs were ignored.

There was another side to Da which we occasionally saw. In company, he could turn on the charm and be incredibly sociable when it suited him. On rare occasions, if he was around when any of our extended family came to visit, he was at his best. He was a master storyteller and could charm the birds off the trees. When he smiled a roguish glint came into his eyes. Even though I wasn't included in these evening gathering, I used to listen from the top of the stairs, and when I heard him holding court like this, it was hard not to be impressed.

Da worked as a porter at Dublin Airport and was very well known and popular with regular travellers, who tipped him handsomely for helping them with their heavy cases. He usually opted for the early shift to have his afternoons free to go to the horse races, leaving our house at 5:30 a.m. He would cycle for an hour to the Cat & Cage pub in Drumcondra, where he parked his bike, and make the rest of his journey on an Aer Lingus courtesy bus, which collected airport staff from the surrounding area. When he was on later shifts, I used to watch him cycle up the street, a formidable sight in his overcoat, Trilby hat and trousers clipped in at the ankles, to protect them from the chain.

There were very few cars on our street when I was a boy, most of the men had similar-looking bikes, except for Mr Kirby's. His chain had a cover, which meant he didn't have to wear clips at the ends of his trousers and the chain itself never came off. It also had a permanent light that was charged by a dynamo as he cycled. This was the best bike on the street and you couldn't but admire it. While Da's bike wasn't as good, he took great care of it, removing the lamp, in case it was stolen when parked outside our front door. At night before going to bed, he used to wheel it into the front room for safety. It would be many years before he would eventually replace this bike with a black Ford Prefect car.

Da hardly ever came home directly from work; he was a gambler and his gambling took precedence over everything. He lived the life of a bachelor and behaved as if he was a visitor in our house. When he arrived home, Ma would set about preparing something for him to eat while he sat at the kitchen table reading his paper. I never heard them talk about family life, it was as if it had nothing to do with him and neither of them ever showed any interest in our education. Sometimes you'd hear Ma say to him "I haven't enough money to last a week, but you can afford to go gambling whenever you want." She couldn't resist taunting him. I suppose she felt safe, with the children around, that he wouldn't fly into a rage.

As an Aer Lingus employee, Da could get cheap tickets for himself and his family, but he never took us on holidays. Every March, while we were growing up, he went off on his own for a month to either Malta or Miami, for the sun and horse racing. One day we came home from school to find Da had returned early from his holiday. He was laid out on the chaise longue in agony, his shirt off and trousers rolled up, covered in huge blisters that looked like jellyfish. Apparently, he had been sheltering from the sun under a tree and fell asleep only to wake up almost burned alive. He had to come home for treatment. We couldn't help but feel sorry for him, that is everyone except Ma. "It serves him right," she said, "He got what he deserved, going

Da in Dublin City 1949

on holidays without his family." The reality was we couldn't have gone anyway, even if invited. We were at school, and she wouldn't have wanted to spend any more time with him than was absolutely necessary. She actually looked forward to his absence during March, and this unexpected early return didn't suit her at all.

Da's March holiday also meant that he missed the twins' and Michael's birthdays —not that they were anything to brag about. When we turned five, my sister and I were each given a present for our big day. Philomena tore the paper off her's immediately and found a metal tea set, with cups, saucers, plates, and cutlery. I was hoping mine would be a gun with caps and was shattered to find a matching tea set. *A tea set for a boy?* I thought. My obvious shock and disappointment provoked a furious response from Ma. "You're never happy, no matter what you get," she said. Needless to say, I never played with that tea set. Birthdays seemed to come and go after that, and we rarely celebrated them as a family.

Christmas, unlike birthdays, was always special at Home Villas. The excitement and anticipation started to build from the first week in December when we decorated the downstairs of the house. We hung balloons, and colourful decorations pulled out like melodeons from corner to corner of the ceilings, creating beautiful shapes. Usually, on our street, heavy curtains would have been drawn in the front rooms in wintertime. In December everyone kept these open to show off the decorations through the lace curtains. Around the middle of the month, fresh holly wreaths were hung on front doors, and Christmas trees went up laden with small lights and sparkling baubles. An air of festivity was building and every morning was special as you came down the stairs into the front room and got a sense of what was to come. By Christmas Eve we could barely contain ourselves, only one more sleep to go.

One Christmas morning, I was about eight and remember racing down the stairs with uncontrollable excitement to see what Santa had brought us. I eagerly picked up my present and ripped the wrapping paper off. I suspected it was a new scooter by the shape, only to find it was my older sister's scooter which had been cleaned up and regifted to me. Absolutely shattered, I looked over at Rita and could see she wasn't exactly happy either, but she never complained or made me feel bad about it. I didn't take that scooter out on the street to ride until well after Christmas because I knew the neighbours would know it was Rita's. The magic of Santa died for me that year!

As children, we got used to not having Da around much, which allowed Ma to take full control of family life at 6 Home Villas. She had the power to make all decisions regarding the house and us, and her word was indisputable. There was no possibility of running to Da for support if we felt unfairly treated. On the rare occasions when he was home during the day, we quickly learned to stay out of his way because it meant he'd run out of gambling money and was reluctantly stuck with us. My Da was an incredibly difficult and complex man. But it isn't lost on me that he was the one to take us on those carefree walks in the park where we could play without strict supervision. He was also the one to give me my first experience of live entertainment and my beloved cinema. I believe he was a better man than Ma made him out, or allowed him to be.

It's hard to understand what brought and kept my parents together. To me, it seemed their marriage was more like an arrangement than a loving relationship. I don't believe my father ever really wanted to be married, but Ma was determined. He told us that they met at a dance, and she swayed his bachelor leanings with the idea of creating a home for him. She enticed him with the prospect of good food and freshly washed and ironed clothes. His desire to have an intimate relationship probably sealed the deal. Back then, in Ireland, contraception was forbidden by the church and so people usually married quickly to unleash their desires. From observing my parents together, I'm more inclined to believe the transactional agreement outweighed any depth of passion between them. There was no big romantic love story behind their union. I never saw any kind of affection between them—no holding hands, no kissing, no hugs, no sleeping in the same room. They lived separate lives under the same roof. They seemed indifferent to each other, until, occasionally, tempers would flare and the fighting would start, causing an underlying current of tension and fear in the house.

Growing up, we were all competing for our parents' attention, learning by example that, when push came to shove, it was every man for himself. This fostered a sad lack of trust and loyalty between my brothers and sisters. We had to find a way to coexist under the same small roof, but there was no chance of forming any lasting bonds.

Joan was the first-born, five years older than me and on the rare occasions when Ma ventured out, she put her in charge of the rest of us. Joan relished being the boss. When we were under her care, it was always "her way" or "no way," just like Ma, and if we didn't follow orders or misbehaved, she was quick to tell on us. Rita, on the other hand, the second oldest girl, four years my senior, was kind and caring, and I loved her. She was full of life and great fun, which meant she was always in trouble with Ma.

Ken, with his big mop of wavy red hair and signature glasses, was the eldest boy, my big brother by three years but in name only. He was Ma and Da's favourite and never got into the same trouble as the rest of us. At school, he was nicknamed "Speedy" and was a popular member

Rita with Michael and myself in Herbert Park 1957

of the running team. His teammates willingly allowed him to ride their bikes around the schoolyard as he didn't have one of his own. One day he invited me to hop up on the crossbar to go for a spin. I was thrilled as we rode up and down until suddenly he lost his balance and we fell against the wall in the yard. My leg got caught on the jagged edge of a tap, which cut a huge gash down my shin. Blood was everywhere. Ken took one look and said, "If you tell Ma about this, I'll never speak to you again", and I said I wouldn't. Nevertheless, when we got home, I couldn't hide my pain or the blood that had congealed in my sock and shoe. When Ma saw the cut, she called the doctor. He told her disapprovingly "this should have been stitched hours ago, but it's too late to do it now." All that was left was to bandage the leg. Ken, true to his word, didn't talk to me for a long while, and as it turned out, we never became close.

Philomena, my twin, and I were the second youngest. Even though we spent a lot of time together as children, I never felt the strong bond between us that twins are supposed to have. Michael was three years younger than us and as might be expected, being the baby of the family, Ma doted on him.

A couple of years after moving into 6 Home Villas, Ma decided it was time to add a lean-to kitchen to the back of the house. Banks didn't lend to people like us, and as this was a costly investment, she must have been squirrelling money away.

We were so eager to see it completed that in the evenings when the builder had gone for the day, we'd sit outside and try to imagine how the kitchen would look. Where everything would go and how grand it would be for all of us.

The reality turned out to be a crudely build construction with a stone floor covered with oilcloth, and it was permanently cold. Where the original wall of the house met the lean-to extension, the window and window sill were left untouched. A long bench was placed against this wall behind a brand-new formica kitchen table where Philomena, Michael, and I used to sit for meals. An ongoing bone of contention between us was who would sit at the uncomfortable end of the bench backing onto the window sill. The roof of the extension was made from corrugated asbestos, and when it rained, it sounded like we were being attacked by thousands of pebbles from overhead. It was so loud that I often thought the roof might cave in. When the water ran down the gutter, it spluttered into the yard and flooded the entire area because there was no drain. The cover for the manhole outside had to be raised slightly to prevent the rainwater flowing into the new kitchen. Great care had to be taken to avoid stepping on it when going outside to the toilet. At least now the toilet was closer to the house, practically indoors as far as we were concerned!

Despite its shortcomings, our new lean-to was now our largest room, running the full twelve-feet width of the house and stretching eight feet out the back. Ma had enough space here to put a large wooden chair with arms and lots of comfortable cushions, from where she could look out the window at her cherished garden. Above this chair, a radio sat on a small shelf, out of bounds to anyone but Ma. When we later got a TV, it was also deemed out of bounds, it was only turned on when Ma and Da wanted to watch something themselves. This was tantalising when other kids were watching their favourite programs, we could only watch whatever our parents wanted.

Having a new kitchen also created space in the scullery for a real bath. Up until then, we used a large galvanised tub for bathing. It would be brought into the back room in front of the fire and then filled with kettles of hot water which were carried from the scullery. I hated having to stand naked in this bath in front of Philomena and Michael. Ma used to wash me vigorously with a large square bar of sunlight soap, the edges digging into my young tender skin. I felt embarrassed by the whole process but had no choice until the extension came along.

Our new bath was a great luxury, with plenty of space to sit down in and no more carrying hot water into the back room. There was a large piece of wood completely covering the bath on which Ma stored an array of things. Clearing this was a lot of trouble, so regular baths were still out of the question. Also, because of its location, people had to pass through it to get to the toilet outside. When we were being washed the doors were left open, to allow access and we used to scream, "Close your eyes!" when anyone walked by. Later, when we got older, we could lock the door until someone started banging it down in desperation to get to the toilet. We'd stall them as long as possible, relishing our precious minutes in the water, knowing it could be some time before we'd get a chance to have a bath again.

Now that we had extra space at the back of the house, Ma decided that the front room would become the "good room". This was for her, and her alone, where she could entertain her very occasional visitors. We had to walk through this room to get to our tiny living space and were under threat not to linger or touch anything. In such a small house, allocating the best living area just for show, was such a waste. It was fitted out with brand new furniture, bought on credit from Drage's department store in Grafton Street and all paid for by weekly instalments, from our already meagre income. It was a ten-by-nine feet room, but she managed to pack in an extendable dining table and six chairs, a sideboard and a display cabinet with glass doors for Ma's cherished Belleek pottery. And last but not least a chaise longue which was only there for show. Ma would rest her arm on this when sitting by the window, observing all the goings-on in the street.

Our newly renovated house was a source of great pride to Ma, so much so, that even our neighbours were invited in to see the finished product—a rare event! As usual, we were under threat to be on our best behaviour and on the surface, we probably seemed like a close and loving family to be envied. No one had any idea what life was like behind our closed doors.

Chapter 2

School is in Session

To ensure there was no chance of us getting too friendly with our neighbours, we were sent to school in the next parish, a solid thirty-minute walk from home. The kids at this school lived too far away to hang around with after school. And with little opportunity to mix with the locals, we weren't in a position to develop any friendships growing up. To add insult to injury, Ma kept us at home as long as possible, presumably for her convenience. This meant Philomena and I were six when we started school, about two years older than most other children.

My first school was the Marian Hall, part of St Anne's Convent School in Milltown. It was a long walk for a six-year-old boy, up Victoria Avenue, then Belmont Avenue, and up the Milltown Road. On my first day, I cried bitterly when Ma went to leave me at the school door. The previous six years with her were all I knew having been cocooned in our house with very limited contact with the world outside. Ma reassured me that she would be waiting there when I came out, so I reluctantly left her side and went in. To my surprise, my new schoolmates were much younger and smaller than me, and the desks were obviously made for this age group as I had to squeeze myself in. That first day seemed endless, and when I came out, true to her word, Ma was there. I was so happy to see her that I ran straight over and threw my arms around her. This public display of affection made her quite uncomfortable, and she quickly pulled away, and we started our journey home. It wasn't long before, Philomena and I were allowed to walk to school with our older siblings, who were attending the school across the road.

During our first year, Philomena and I had to prepare for our First Holy Communion and joined in with the boys and girls in the higher class who were the same age as us. The nuns explained the significance of this important milestone in our lives and the fact that only those who had confessed their sins and received Holy Communion could go directly to heaven. They tried to explain the difference between mortal and venial sins, and the associated penalties if we were to commit either. But the whole concept was lost on me. We spent hours learning prayers by heart. And in preparation for taking Holy Communion itself, we practised with pieces of ice cream wafer, which used to get stuck to the roof of my mouth. We were warned against letting the "host" touch our teeth before swallowing, as it represented the body and blood of Our Lord Jesus Christ. Pretty stressful!

After all the preparations, what I remember most about my Communion Day was the party we had in the school hall and calling to the neighbour's houses with Philomena to collect money. It was a novelty, twins making their first holy communion, and our "collections" reflected this. We showed off our outfits, and everyone made us feel so special. Later in the day, we visited our relatives and, by the time we got home, my pockets were bulging with threepenny and sixpenny pieces. That evening I emptied the coins onto the table and stacked them in piles. It was a glorious sight. Before I knew it, it was time to go to bed. I never saw that money again!

It wasn't until after my communion that my life at school took its first real turn for the worse. Arithmetic was easy for me, but all hell broke loose when I put a pencil in my hand and attempted "joined-up" writing. As I diligently tried to copy what the nun had just written on the board, I noticed her looking at me strangely. Next thing I knew, she was standing by my desk and was furiously pulling the pencil out of my hand. "You're writing with the wrong hand," she said abruptly, forcing the pencil into my other hand. "This is the hand you write with," she added.

The Twins First Holy Communion 1956

I didn't understand why she was saying this because I was using the hand that came naturally to me. Terrified of disobeying her, I tried to write, but keeping the letters within the lines was impossible. So I put the pencil back in my left hand. This infuriated her. "It's evil to write with your left hand!" she said angrily and pulled the pencil out of my hand again. I didn't know what she was talking about. Next thing she grabbed my left arm and forced it down the back of my trousers. "Leave that hand there until we're finished writing" she ordered in a shrill voice. Pain crept up my fingers and past my elbow, cramping my entire arm. I remained still while the rest of the class quietly chuckled at my predicament. Soon my right hand started to cramp as well, as I struggled to control the pencil and do my best to write. Frustrated, humiliated and hurt, I released my left hand and went back to what was natural for me.

"Stand up, Patrick Lee," resounded the nun's terrifying voice from the front of the class. Then she called the whole class to attention."Stop writing, everyone, and listen carefully to me. Children who write with their left hands are evil. The devil chooses them to do his work," she declared. I was shocked! Of course, at seven years of age, I believed what she was saying. After all, she worked directly for God. All I could think was, *Part of me is evil? How can this be? I've just made my Communion. What's happening to me?* "You all need to help me to do God's work," the nun demanded. "Whenever you see Patrick writing with his left hand, tell me, because we've got to save him for God." So, placed under their watchful eyes, my classmates were only too eager to diligently report on me. And as if this humiliation wasn't bad enough, every time I wrote with my left hand, the nun would furiously hit me on the knuckles with a ruler. I never told my family what was happening, I didn't want them to know I was evil. For the same reason, I never confessed to the priest. Under this severe pressure, I was trained to use my right hand for writing, but for everything else, I remained a lefty. The damage caused by the physical and mental cruelty of the nuns has been permanent. Even now that I am free to write with whichever hand I want, there is a mental block that doesn't allow me to revert back to what was once natural for me.

I left the Marian Hall when I was eight to attend St. Gaul's Boys National School in the same parish. It was here that my difficulties with spelling and reading surfaced. Despite now having to write with my right hand, I managed to do a good job copying down letters from the blackboard. But when I was asked to put the letters together to form words, it was all mumbo jumbo to me. And when I tried to read, it was like looking at a plate of Alphabetti Spaghetti, with all the letters jumbled up. The only way I could deal with this was to look for groups of letters that made some sense to me, and then guess what the rest of the words were.

On most occasions, my guesswork failed me. Every day I'd wait anxiously, knowing that at some stage the teacher's eyes would land on me and I'd be picked out to read aloud. It wasn't long before that dreaded day came and I heard my name called out, "Padraig O'Laogh read from page ten." (at this school we were always called by the Irish version of our names). As I stood up with the open book in my hand, clearly paralysed with fear, I heard the teacher say to the class, "This should be good." The whole class burst into laughter and any chance of me being able to make sense of the mixed-up letters on the page in front of me vanished. "OK, read just one line, go on, just one line," the teacher taunted, encouraging the class to continue jeering and laughing at me. I was gripped with anxiety and said nothing. I just stood there, embarrassed, humiliated and unable to defend myself. "Ah, you're a lost cause," the teacher said abruptly and moved on to the next student. My spirit was crushed. The screams in my head started tormenting me as I began that familiar mental journey of falling into a bottomless pit of despair. I couldn't escape myself.

Sometimes the teacher got so frustrated that he pulled me up in front of the whole class and gave me "six of the best." He would lift the cane high in the air and bring it down repeatedly on

37

my palms, brandishing it as if it was a sword, crisscrossing from side to side. My instinct was to pull away, but that proved to be a fatal mistake because when I did, the boys started to laugh infuriating the teacher. He doubled the number of slaps and this time, he held my wrists firmly. The pain was like a sting, searing and sharp, taking my breath away with each swipe, but as I walked back to my seat, I vowed never to let them see me cry.

I channelled all my powerlessness and frustration in seething curses carefully muttered under my breath so as not to get into even more trouble. *"You fat, bald coward, you know nothing about me, I hope you rot in hell,"* I whispered to myself, wishing I could scream it in his face. After many months, I learned to cope with the canings. When the teacher realised he was not having the desired impact, he started to lift me up by my sideburns. The pain was like nothing I had known before and, to his advantage, it left no marks. I will never forget the sadistic look on his face as he forced me to rise up on my tippy toes in agony or the sympathetic glances from my classmates. Watching this barbaric abuse was not for the faint-hearted.

At home, because no one had any interest in how I was doing, my learning issues went unnoticed. Until one day, I finally gathered the courage to speak up and ask for some help. I told Ma how unfair and brutal the teacher was being, but she chose to take his side. "Listen," she said dismissively "they wouldn't be

School Photo - my first year at St Gauls 1958

slapping you for no reason, you probably deserved it, I can't do anything to help you." I tried desperately to get my point across, hoping she'd believe me and come to my rescue, but to no avail. My persistence had the opposite effect: I frustrated and annoyed her so much, she gave me a beating to shut me up for good. That was the end of that as far as she was concerned. I was at fault, no one else was to blame. I was a slow child, unable to grasp the fundamentals of reading and writing, impossible to teach. So I had to accept their collective diagnosis and reluctantly took my place as the dunce of the class.

So each school morning I got up, ate my breakfast, and headed off on my walk to that dreaded place. I counted each step I took to distract me from thinking about what lay ahead, always hoping that today would be the day when things got better. Once I got to school, the days seemed endless. I kept an eye on the hands of the clock on the classroom wall and felt growing relief as it ate away the minutes until it was time to go home. Eventually, the teacher stopped asking me anything, permanently labelling me a "lost cause" and ignoring my existence.

When the teachers weren't shunning me, it was my classmates who took it upon themselves to make me feel like an outcast. They were all in their own established groups from local neighbourhoods, while I was the only one from Donnybrook. I was also two years older than them, and as the dunce of the class, not a desirable member of any of their groups. Eventually, I decided to run home for lunch to avoid the growing despair; it was better than hanging around the schoolyard on my own with nothing to do.

In a desperate attempt to somehow fit in at school, I always tried to look neat and tidy. If my shirt was dirty, and I asked Ma to wash it, she always replied: "It's not washing day." So rather than put the dirty shirt back on, I used to turn it inside out. I assumed it looked better that way, though it was hard to judge the full effect as the only mirror available at home was my Da's small shaving mirror. Putting on a shirt inside out is not as easy as it might seem. It was really difficult to button from the outside and try to hide, with my tie, the fact that the buttons were on the wrong side. I used to push the shirt into my trousers and even into my underpants to secure it and give it an ironed appearance, never thinking about the clearly visible inside seams. I'm sure I looked ridiculous. The lads at school must have had a great laugh "not only is he illiterate, but he can't even dress!"

Sport helped somewhat to alleviate those tortuous schooldays. Like most young boys, I loved playing ball games and jumped at any rare chance, Ma allowed us to play outside with the neighbours. Occasionally Da would take us to Herbert Park for a game of hurling. But when we played with him, we spent most of the time running and collecting his long shots—he

41

seldom allowed us to have the hurley stick. The game would last until he got bored and we then walked back home exhausted and frustrated. This didn't diminish my love of the game, especially since Da often mentioned that we came from the County of hurlers, famously called the Kilkenny Cats.

At St Gaul's, Gaelic football and hurling were the school sports, and my older brother Ken was part of the hurling team. One day Ma asked Ken to bring me along with him to practice, as she had to go out and would not be home until late. During the hurling practice, the teacher asked if I would like to have a go playing. Hurling was in my blood, so of course, I said yes and off I went onto the field. I naturally took the stick in my left hand, and this made it very difficult for anyone to get the ball from me. When I hit it in the air, it seemed to travel for miles. I had a great time, and the coach was so impressed that he invited me to join the school team. I was over-the-moon excited and so proud to think that I might be carrying the Kilkenny hurling gene. Finally, I had something to look forward to at school, something I was good at! I couldn't wait to get home and ask Ma. But she said no, the playing pitch, one mile away from school in the opposite direction of our house, was too far away, she explained. Ken was three years older than me, so making his way home wasn't an issue, but I was too young. My heart sank. I finally had an opportunity to shine and demonstrate that the one who everyone called "useless" could excel at something. No amount of pleading would change her mind, her decision was final.

Everyone in the class was moving forward, but I seemed to be at a dead end, and couldn't get out of the malaise. The harder I tried learning to read, the more confusing it got. And when put under pressure, I had no hope at all of making out the words in front of me. For the next few years, I just sat in class, watching everyone pass me by. My teachers seemed clueless about how to help me. No one seemed to care that I was in their class, but not part of it. No one cared enough to try and teach me, but they continued to pass me on to the next grade regardless. So I was moving along with no real education to show for those years of living hell. I had no choice but to accept my fate, and against my nature to be sociable, I became quite introverted. My lust for life and deep routed competitive streak had to be buried. I wanted to find out so much about everything around me, but my hunger for knowledge went unsatisfied. There was no one there to help, and after all those painful years of schooling, the only education I got was what I could see with my own two eyes. It would be years before I was diagnosed with dyslexia which left me feeling total contempt for those teachers, who failed me on so many levels - bullies with impunity.

Chapter 3

The Magic Life on our Street

Watching what was going on up and down our street was spectacular for a curious, lost and lonely young boy like me. Surrounding us was a constant hive of activity, with traders coming and going each week. It was on this street that the first seeds of my interest in business were firmly planted. I was fascinated and completely absorbed by the dealings and banter between the traders and customers, the bargaining, the back and forth, as they went about selling their wares.

There was Milkman Larry, selling milk from the shiny gold and silver churns on his horse and cart. Women came out in their aprons, porcelain jugs in hand and gathered around the back of the horse and cart to wait their turn. Larry would open the tap on the churn and let the delicious fresh milk flow into the jugs with a familiar gushing sound. Freshly laid eggs could also be bought from him, in ones, twos, or threes, and these fit neatly into the women's apron pockets. While this was going on, the ladies chatted among themselves, catching up on all the local news and gossip and they remained on the street long after the milk cart had gone. All except Ma, that was who thought this was beneath her. She had Larry come to our door, to pick up her jug or if I was around, she'd ask me to do it. This used to embarrass me. I felt it was insulting to our neighbours who were always very friendly to me.

Milkman Larry also kept pigs in his small farmyard just up the road, and he called to the street every week for "slops" to feed them. Each house provided their own slop buckets, usually an old cooking oil tin with a handle, and more importantly a lid to keep the smells in. We stored ours under the sink in the kitchen, which was handy for Ma. Larry came to the door himself to collect the buckets and carry them to the large steel container which, on this occasion, replaced the milk churns on his cart. Everyone was happy to do Larry a favour and get rid of their smelly food waste at the same time.

On Wednesdays and Saturdays, there was another opportunity for the women to catch up when Christy came by on his much bigger horse and cart selling fruit and vegetables. He'd park at the top of the street, around the bend on Auburn Road, and everyone would come up to the cart to shop. I loved watching Christy in action, exchanging kind greetings, cheerfully and efficiently meeting everyone's needs and then moving swiftly on

46

to the next customer. It was part of our weekly routine at Home Villas, but it never ceased to amaze me.

The gas man came twice a month to collect the money from the meters. He would come into our house, open the meter, take out the cash box, and empty it onto the table. The speed at which he counted the coins was impressive. As he quickly swiped the shillings from the table into his hand, he set all foreign coins aside. Da used to get tips in the airport, sometimes in foreign currency that happened to be the exact size of a shilling. Ma used these foreign coins in the meter when money was short, knowing that she would have to replace them later when the gas man came to collect. Yet, the gas man always left the foreign coins on the table in case we needed them again, so we were never out of gas.

The fishmonger was another sight to behold when he came on Fridays. He had a reliable customer base on our street, as this was the day the Catholic Church had forbidden its flock to eat meat. Women came with their plates in hand, chose their fish whole, and unless they had a cat to feed, asked to have it filleted on the spot "ready for the pan." Salmon was not in high demand because of the high price, but for some reason, I still remember those beautiful pink cutlets with silver skins. I had no desire to get too close to the proceedings because, although I loved watching him go through the motions of gutting and deboning, I didn't like the taste of fish and least of all the smell of it.

Bin day was also on Friday when all the metal bins from the street were placed out front on the path for collection. Ours was usually kept in the back behind the coal shed, and it was the children's job to carry them through the house. Holding one handle each, we moved as fast as we could, making sure the lid was held down firmly so the smell wouldn't linger in the house. When the bin men arrived, they emptied the trash into their lorry and, as they went along, cleaned up any debris on the street with a shovel and brush. The clattering sound of the lids hitting the pavement was the signal that the trash had been collected, it was time to take the bins in. Whoever brought them in had to wash out the smelly remains, so this was not an envied task.

Wintertime brought with it the coal man. He carried big bags of coal on his shoulder, through the houses, to the outside coal sheds. As he lowered the bag and emptied it, you could hear the crash on the ground and see the black dust rising. He was always covered in coal dust from head to toe. But of all the men who called to the street, there was none dirtier or caused more disruption, than the chimney sweeper. No matter what precautions were taken to protect the house from the soot, it still managed to get everywhere, and it took days to clean up and get rid of the pungent smell.

Among the other regular traders to call on Home Villas was the bread man, from Johnston Mooney and O'Brien. When his van doors opened, the glorious smell of fresh bread wafted through the air along the street, enticing his customers to come out and buy. The paper man came every day at five o'clock, loudly announcing his arrival with repeated cries of "Herald or Press, Press or Herald." There was also a weekly Street Singer, who sang for tips. And a knife sharpener who came much less frequently, fascinating us with the extra pedal on his bike which rotated the knife sharpener. We also had priests and nuns come by occasionally, looking for money. If spotted early enough, you could pretend you weren't in—these visitors were to be avoided whenever possible.

Our corporation street was spoiled with the multiplicity of products and services brought directly to our front doors. We didn't have to go anywhere. Even the rent man called to collect the weekly dues. However, there is no doubt we were the worker bees of the city. We were educated and trained to do only menial tasks and not progress from our station in life. This could have brought the collective morale down. But we were united in poverty and pulled together to create a vibrant community. One that Ma rarely participated in, and I desperately wanted to be part of.

One local religious event that sticks out in my mind is the annual May procession through the streets of Donnybrook. May was the month of Our Lady, the Mother of God, and this procession was a highlight for the local community. People came in their droves to express their devotion and to view the spectacular show. The village was adorned with bunting, strung from lamp post to lamp post along the procession route, and loudspeakers bellowed out hymns such as the well known "Bring Flowers of the Fairest".

The priests led the procession, in all their finery, one of them carrying an incense burner which released a distinct pungent smell as he swung it in the shape of a cross. Following behind were church deacons, altar boys and nuns. Then came the local politicians, policemen, nurses, scouts and other representatives from various community groups. They were dressed in their uniforms or "Sunday Best", and all radiated a sense of elevated smugness. Children, in their new communion outfits, walked proudly by with their classmates and teachers. I wasn't allowed to take part in the procession because I didn't go to school in the parish, but Ma used to bring us up to the village to show our respect and to be seen. We often stood in one spot for two hours as the colourful groups filed by and later when I became an altar boy in Donnybrook church, I was able to join in.

Prisoners of Ma's anxiety, most days, when we were home from school, we were confined to the house or our garden. When she did relent and let us out to play on the street, it was a real treat and cause for celebration. It gave me a chance to mix with children who knew nothing about my difficulties at school. Since we rarely came out, it was a novelty for them too, and they willingly allowed us to join in their games of soccer, hopscotch, skipping, and marbles. We would take off our jumpers to form goalposts, and the curb would act as the touchline for our improvised soccer matches. Ropes were tied to lampposts to create swings—not very sophisticated contraptions, but they served their purpose and were great fun. And when the odd car drove down the street, we quickly scattered in fear for our lives but were soon back in position enjoying our games as if nothing had happened.

Having this facility to play, just outside our door, meant that Ma could keep an eye on us at all times. The rule was never to move off the street, and therefore the adjacent Herbert Park was definitely out of bounds unless she was with us. When it was time to come in, we had clear instructions not to knock on the front door. She used to leave the front window open a few inches so we could call in to her. This way, she knew it was just us and not a stranger and would open the door.

Ma sometimes took us to Herbert Park, but we had to stay within her eyeshot at all times and were not allowed to mix with other children. I used to occupy myself collecting chestnuts, and jumping on and off the walls and steps. My older siblings weren't interested in playing, Michael was too small, and Philomena was a girl! There were usually local kids playing only a few feet away, and it was difficult not to join in their games. But there was no question of disobeying Ma when she said something, she meant it. If I ever dared go against her, with just one look from her, I knew I was in trouble. I would spend the rest of the day trying to please her, sitting by her side, telling her how sorry I was, pleading with her to talk to me and not be so angry. But all she'd say was, "Wait 'till I get you home and we'll see how sorry you are!" Sometimes she'd let me off in the end, but with the threat hanging over me for so long, the day was already ruined.

On Saturdays Ma usually went to Drages in Grafton Street, to make the weekly higher purchase payment for our "good" furniture. She used to combine this with some shopping on Chatham Street, and if she needed help to carry the shopping, she'd often ask for my help. She would take me with her up to the bus stop in the village and tell me to wait there and count the buses until she got back. I counted so many buses come and go that the drivers got to know me and would salute me as they passed by on their round trip. To keep myself busy, I also counted the number of Ford cars that passed by or measured the distance between the five redbrick houses behind the bus stop, heel to toe, heel to toe. This required focus, which I often lost when another bus appeared in the distance and distracted me. Sometimes I'd sit on the low redbrick wall that cordoned off the front gardens with my back against the ornate black railings, while people-watching on the busy treelined street. On rainy days I took shelter under a large tree beside the bus stop but getting wet was unavoidable as the big drops from the water-laden branches fell down on me.

Since Ma had told me not to move from the bus stop, I daren't slip home, even though our house was only five minutes away. When I needed to pee, I used to run down to the lane behind the nearby house to do my business and rush back in fear that I may have missed her arrival. She would have been gone for about two to three hours and, as every bus stopped, I peered at the line of people getting off, hoping she would be among them. Sometimes a neighbour who had gone to town earlier, and seen me at the stop, would return before Ma, and ask sardonically, "Is your ma not home yet?" To which I would reply, "No, but she'll be on the next bus." Even though this probably wasn't true, I didn't want them to think badly of Ma and hated to see the fake sympathy in their eyes.

Band Performance in Herbert Park.

Michael, Philomena, Ma & me. 1957

Chapter 4

She gave me life, never her smile.

I often wished I had been adopted. This would have explained so much. In my young mind, that would have helped justify my parents' distant and cruel behaviour, but I had no such luck. Once Philomena and I hit school age, things began to deteriorate at home. Ma's fear of what we might do beyond the door of our house, far from her watchful eye, was so great that she began firmly laying down the law. It was as if her little angels were suddenly little devils in her eyes.

One afternoon, I noticed boys playing marbles just outside our house, so I pestered her to let me go outside to watch them. Reluctantly, she gave in, and I gleefully ran out to catch a glimpse of the game. When I went to head back inside, I called out and knocked on the window, but there was no answer. As I hadn't seen her leave, I knew she was inside. I kept knocking and calling and then Ma's previous threat began to reverberate loudly in my head. *"I will put you outside the door,"* she said. *"What will you do then? Where will you go? Where will you sleep?"*

Was this it then? Was this the day she'd lock me out for good? I was only a boy, how could she be so cruel? My calls turned to desperate crying, pleading her to let me in. Twenty minutes later, she finally walked to the door and opened it. Trembling with fear, I scampered in and cowered in the corner of the room. I glanced at Ma for reassurance, but all I got in return was her stone-cold glare. "I told you I'd lock you out," she said viscously, as she turned her back on me and walked out into the kitchen. I followed her in and begged her on my knees to forgive me. "Just look at yourself," she said with disdain. At that moment, I felt so bad about belittling myself in a pathetic attempt to appeal to her, that it would take me years to forgive myself and overcome the feeling of shame. Ma used this threat of locking me out to keep me under her control, and it worked. She had purposefully broken my spirit.

Even though Ma controlled us rigidly and insisted on keeping us inside as much as possible, our presence seemed to bother her. During the school year, twenty minutes at lunchtime was manageable and probably a welcome recess in her lonely day. But by the time we were all home later in the afternoon, she imposed a strict bedtime policy on us three younger children.

After six o'clock, we were not to be seen or heard downstairs even when we had visitors coming. "I have visitors coming, and want you in bed before they get here," she'd say, "If you're good, I'll bring you up a party, when they're gone." This was usually a slice of apple and an orange wedge for each of us. Not much but better than nothing. Any hint of complaint from us was stopped short immediately, so we followed her orders. When I'd hear the knock on the door and the warm greetings below, I'd carefully open the bedroom door and sit on the small landing listening to the chat.

One evening I heard my aunt ask, "Where are the kids?" and Ma replied, "Oh, they're up in bed, they're sleeping, they were out all day." I couldn't believe my ears and didn't understand why we were being excluded from the family fun. So I quietly returned to our room, carefully shut the door, and enviously endured all the laughter echoing from downstairs. Ma always oozed with kindness when any of her family were around. There was nothing she wouldn't do for them. Her pièce de résistance was when she gave them her good-luck rub. "There's a bit of good luck for you," she'd say and "hey presto" they'd immediately feel the better for it. This "rub" was highly sought after by all of us, and there was no doubt in anyone's mind that Ma had the power. Over the years, I watched her bestow this gift on her favourite people. But when I asked for it, she said no, humiliating me in front of Michael and Philomena. I was so sorry I asked, I never asked again.

So, every evening at six sharp, the three of us were confined to our small bedroom room overlooking Herbert Park. We had three hours to kill before being tired enough to fall asleep. That was torture, especially when the weather was good. The sounds from outside pierced through the window and echoed in our room. We could hear the kids laughing and playing in the park right beyond our garden wall. Meanwhile, we were stuck in that stifling room with the curtain drawn because heaven forbid any of the kids would see us. Every now and then, we'd defy our mother's strict orders and crawl over to the window, peel the curtain back slightly and peer out at all the fun we were missing. If anyone looked up at our window, we would quickly close the curtain, duck down under the window sill, and hope to God that we hadn't been seen. We wouldn't want them to know we were confined to our bedroom. To make things worse, with no access to the downstairs toilet, we had to use a potty. And if used, the room became filled with a nauseating stench.

My smelly shoes and socks didn't help with the stench, so I'd put them outside on the window sill to air overnight. If it happened to rain overnight, I'd wring out the socks from the bedroom window onto the corrugated roof below and then put them on. I didn't mind the wet socks because they cooled my feet, which were always roasting hot. I don't know how I didn't get sick, but at the time I found it incredibly refreshing, and no one warned me it wasn't a good idea. Windy nights were more worrying because if my shoes and socks blew off the window sill, I had to climb down the next morning onto the kitchen roof to retrieve them. In time, I learned how to secure my socks by wedging them between the window and its frame. Once we got older, Michael and I were moved in with Da and Ken to the front bedroom overlooking the street, which meant I had to leave my shoes and socks in the backyard before going up to bed. None of this really made much of a difference, though. In the end, every day I was putting on old, smelly socks and shoes, trying to fool myself into believing they were a little fresher after their night out.

To help pass the time and entertain ourselves during those long evening confined to our bedroom, Philomena and I would start chitchatting and joking around. This inevitably gave way to stifled giggles that turned into outright laughter. Once we crossed that line, we'd start playing around and jumping from bed to bed, unaware of how this raucous resonated in the floor below. We were kids, we were trying to have fun despite our circumstances. It was all great until we'd stop cold with the foreboding sound of the broom handle banging on the ceiling below. That dreaded signal immediately silenced us, because we knew the detrimental outcome if we continued. But after about a half-hour, our fear would subside, and the fun and bickering would resurface. And then the worst sounds of all: the terrifying pounding footsteps climbing up the stairs, stopping only to remove a triangular wooden stair rod from its clips. That could only be one person: Ma. She'd barge into the room, the two of us stricken with sheer terror, and then grab us one by one, pull up the nightdress or pull down the pyjama bottoms, and start whacking our bare skin with the rod. Michael, an innocent bystander, was terrified as he watched these horrific punishments. Philomena's piercing screams still ring in my ears, and the image of Ma delivering her beatings with such fury and coldness will never be erased from my mind.

As soon as she was done, she'd walk out and bang the door behind her, leaving us gasping for air between sobs to calm our traumatised bodies. When at long last our bitter tears subsided, we'd emerge from the fog of shock, exchange glances, and begin to whisper to and fro:

"She hit me harder than she hit you."

"No, she did not."

"She did, I know she did."

"Well, let's see?"

"Oh yeah, your marks look much worse than mine," one would say to the other as we compared the red lines across our bodies. Then we'd crawl into bed and try to sleep it off. That is unless the beating came early in the evening when we'd dry our tears and eventually start chitchatting again. Distracted by whatever new game we'd come up with, we would forget about the risk we were taking, until we could hear the familiar thundering sound of steps on the stairs. Those twice-beaten nights were the worst. Such was the traumatising legacy of those beatings that, to this day, I lock my bedroom door for fear of being caught off guard by anyone.

There were other traumatic boyhood experiences, such as visits to the hospital, that also stick in my mind. Once I was brought to Baggot Street Hospital with severe back pain after over stretching to reach something on the table at teatime. I suddenly screamed in agony and could barely move with the pain. My parents quickly rushed me out the door, up the street, and onto the first bus to the hospital, a journey from hell. The pain was so excruciating that I had to stand all the way there. The doctor at the hospital told my parents that he knew what was wrong and how to fix it. But he didn't address me directly, not even with his eyes even though I was screaming in pain right next to him. Once we had seen the doctor, I was brought, with my parents, into a room and put up on an iron bed. A nurse proceeded to place straps very tightly around my shoulders, under my arms, and around my legs

61

and ankles. The straps appeared to be connected to what looked like a clock face with a big handle. The doctor then began to turn the handle slowly, and I could feel my body being pulled apart. I screamed and cried to no avail. I thought I was going to die; it felt like they were actually pulling me apart. When it was all over, everyone was happy except me. The sharp pain was gone but in its place was anger. They had all allowed me to go through so much terror without explaining what was happening. I refused to say goodbye to the doctor, and my parents gave out to me all the way home. It took me weeks to get the images out of my mind.

Another hospital experience I will never forget is when I had my tonsils and adenoids taken out. Ma brought me to the Eye and Ear Hospital and told me I had to stay there. I had no idea this was related to my sore throat. Again things were never explained to me. I felt abandoned and cried myself to sleep. Early the next morning, I woke with the noise of my bed being wheeled down a corridor. Suddenly a mask was placed over my mouth, and my immediate reaction was to pull it off. The smell of gas was awful. The next thing I remember I was back in the ward, my throat aching in pain. Ma was there, but she could do nothing to ease the pain every time I tried to swallow. For the next two days, I lay in a ward with no other children, only old men. They laughed and talked crudely among themselves, ignoring me, as if I wasn't there. I refused to eat anything until a stern nurse told me that I would not be allowed home unless I did. When the lunch tray arrived, I forced the food down my throat, despite the searing pain. All I wanted to do was go home.

Where was Da, while all this went on? Either at work or gambling. For as long as I can remember, Da went to every race meeting in the country and also played poker regularly. Ma told us that he used to be a heavy drinker and smoker as well, but gave up both in favour of gambling. When there wasn't a race meeting to go to, he did his gambling in betting shops (commonly known as bookies). He liked to distribute his bets between several of these, to keep a certain level of anonymity. When this was the local bookie, Ma used to send me up to tell him his dinner was ready. Children were not allowed inside these shops, so I would have to whisper loudly from the doorway, "Daaaa, Da, your dinner is ready. Ma says to come home." All heads would turn to see who was being summoned, which would infuriate my father. I hated having to do this for fear he would get mad at me, so I would run home ahead of him to escape his anger. There was always a row with Ma when he walked through the door, but she must have felt it was worth it to embarrass him in front of his fellow gamblers. I didn't realise at the time that she was using me to get at him. This was a tactic she often employed, not caring who got caught in the crossfire.

One day, unaware Da was home, I rushed into the boys' bedroom, creating a draft as I opened the door. I was suddenly surrounded by money flying all over the place. "Holy mother of God!" Da shouted, "What are you doing?" Startled by his voice, I stopped short and couldn't believe my eyes: there was money everywhere, falling like confetti. As he got up and began to gather up the notes, I bent over to help him, but Da shouted angrily, "Don't touch them! I'll do it." "Ah, Da," I pleaded, " let me help." "Stay back," he said firmly, gathering the notes together in a pile on the bed. "Wow," I uttered in amazement. "How much is there?" "Eighteen hundred pounds," he said, with a wry smile briefly replacing his scowl.

I had never seen so much money in all my life. But sadly, within days, it was all gone. Da had, more than likely gambled it all away and was now moping around the house in a foul mood. As I grew older and became all too aware of the value of money, I realised that Da's big win could have bought six of our houses outright. We could have been rich! But with gamblers, money feeds the addiction that gives them their adrenaline rush and, in most cases, the Bookmaker ends up being the winner. Sometimes Da gave Ma a pound note or a fiver from his winnings, but we were always short of money, and she bitterly resented the waste of money on his addiction.

Unsurprisingly, it was Da who taught me how to play draughts and cards. He was skilled at both and highly competitive, even with his own kids. During a game, it would sometimes appear as if one of us might get the upper hand, but this never happened. Da always emerged as the winner leaving us feeling frustrated and wanting to play another game in the hope that this time it would be our turn to win. The upside of all of this was that I became very skilled myself at drafts. I have had many hours of enjoyment playing over the years. Poker was also something I eventually mastered and gave me a captivating adrenaline rush each time I played. Gambling was clearly in my blood, but because of my experience of the devastating impact it had on my family, I reluctantly gave it up. I couldn't take the risk of becoming a compulsive gambler myself.

Da was also the one who first took me to the Royal Theatre in town. I was around ten or eleven, and he surprised the younger ones by bringing us to see a live variety show. I had no idea what to expect, and when the curtains opened, we were gobsmacked. The show was spectacular, and the music from the live orchestra seated down in the pit in front of the stage was thrilling. There were comedians, singers, and trapeze artists who took our breath away with their death-defying acts. We were enthralled. The audience went wild, applauding enthusiastically. And just when I thought it couldn't get any better, out came the famous Royalettes, the highlight of the whole event. The excitement in the theatre went up another notch when these ten fabulous dancers appeared. With arms linked, they swayed in unison from side to side kicking their legs high in the air, to the spontaneous appreciation of the audience. The atmosphere was euphoric, and by the end of it all, we were exhausted from all the excitement. This was my first experience of live performance, never to be forgotten.

A side of Da, which was hard to fathom, was his quirky sense of humour. For instance, one day, he took Michael, Philomena and me on a long walk toward town, not telling us where we were going. Our excitement grew with every step in anticipation of what treat might be in store for us. We stopped right outside the Capital Cinema, and my heart skipped a beat, assuming we were going to the pictures. Then Da walked us up the steps, into the foyer, and immediately turned and walked us out the other side. "You can tell your Ma you were at the pictures," he said with a smirk on his face. He seemed to think this was funny. "Ah, come on, Da, come on," we pleaded. But suddenly his tone changed, and we knew there was no chance of us going. We were bitterly disappointed and walked the long journey home in silence, all the worst for the experience.

He also used to tease us with a ruse about finding money in the park. As we walked along, he would sometimes point to the ground about three feet ahead and say, "Jesus, what's that?" We would race ahead to see what it was, but he always managed to barge his way through and get there before us, picking up a silver coin. He'd carefully examine the coin as if he didn't know what it was, and before placing it in his pocket, would kiss it and declare, "That's a bit of good luck." This happened so often, we were stunned at how luck always seemed to be on his side, until one day I noticed him flipping a coin forward before the start of this shenanigan.

On another of our walks in Herbert Park, three air hostesses in their green uniforms passed us by. They recognised Da and greeted him as they approached, "Canice, how are you, are these your kids?" He replied, "No, I don't know who they are. I gave them a few sweets, and they won't stop following me." We were taken back by these comments and, when we got home, Philomena relayed the whole incident to Ma. "He denied us, he denied us!" she told her, obviously very upset. By now, I was getting used to his insensitive sense of humour.

These were all jokes Da played on us when he was in good spirits. When he was in a bad mood, there was nowhere safe. All you could hope for was that you weren't at the butt of his anger. We had seen his vicious temper erupt when Ma went too far with her belittling verbal digs. This terrified us all, including

Ma. When his temper abated, she would act the injured party and give him the silent treatment, prolonging the tension for days.

I remember one day, and I was in the kitchen with Michael, Philomena and Ken when Ma and Da started arguing. However, this time the tone was more severe and their argument turned into a screaming match. Then Da started to push Ma while she tried to defend herself. But Da was towering over her and forced her back into the scullery. We looked on horrified, begging him to stop. I was screaming and wailing so loudly that the sound of my voice terrified me. Next thing, Ma fell against the bath and down onto the floor with a loud thud. We were hysterical when we saw her lying flat out. I thought he'd killed her; I thought she was dead. I could feel myself nervously and uncontrollably stepping backwards and forward. "Leave her alone!" I was screaming, not knowing what else to do.

Suddenly Ken ran to the kitchen and pulled out a potato masher from the cutlery drawer. He rushed into the scullery and hit Da over the head with it. Clearly dumbfounded, Da stopped dead in his tracks and noticed blood trickling down his face. He grabbed the nearest towel, patting his head to stop the bleeding and left the house immediately. We remained still for a few minutes, paralysed by what we had just witnessed. Da had beaten our Ma up, but she was still breathing; she was still alive. Seeing the terror in our eyes, she slowly gathered herself and stood up.

"I'm all right, I'm all right" she kept repeating as she tried to calm us. We cried for hours. I had been at the receiving end of Da's bad temper when he forced me to eat the egg whites when I was only six. But this was different, the rage he had cooped up inside erupted like a violent volcano. I had never felt such terror or helplessness, my innocence was lost, and I was scarred for life. On that day, I vowed to myself never to give him any reason to beat me up, and I was able to keep this promise and hold him off for several years to come.

The house was quiet for the next few days. Everybody tiptoed around what was no longer a safe haven. At night there was silence in our bedroom. Our mother had been hurt, and Philomena, Michael, and I were not going to add to her pain by being rowdy. As for my big brother Ken, although we didn't have a good relationship, on that occasion, I was proud and grateful to him. He had saved Ma from what I believed, as a young boy, could have been her death. When Da returned to the house, we were all in bed, and he was gone to work by the time we got up. It would be three days before we would see him again when to our surprise, he called us all into the back room. Out of the blue, he presented Ma with a box of Cadbury chocolates which he insisted she open there and then. I noticed that the cellophane wrapper was already torn off and wondered why. It became clear when she lifted the lid, and there were about twenty, or thirty-pounds in notes, piled on top of the chocolates. This worked wonders for Ma. She put the cash in her apron pocket, and we all sat down and ate the delicious chocolates. Ma and Da were reconciled, which was a great relief, but I was traumatised for life.

Chapter 5

Summertimes

Summertime was my happy time. When school broke for the summer holidays, there was a great sense of relief and optimism. Although we had to go back in September, this was a lifetime away and not even worth the thought. There was so much to look forward to, starting off with ice cream! If Da happened to be at home on a hot sunny day, he would sometimes send Philomena and me down to Ballsbridge, to get eight ice cream cones for the family. This was about a fifteen-minute walk through Herbert Park. He warned us not to lick them before we got home, because if we did, he wouldn't give us one.

We set out on our mission delighted, only to feel the real pressure land when we had our hands carefully wrapped around the cones, and we began our journey back home. Under the hot sun, the ice cream immediately began to melt and run down our fingers and onto our wrists. Even though we were tempted, we never licked the cones, thinking our Da would surely notice. So we quickened our pace on the long walk home, passing playing fields, tennis courts and the duck pond, avoiding collisions with other kids playing and dogs running by us. We then faced the eighteen narrow steps that would bring us closer to our destination. We climbed each one carefully, focusing on our precious cargo, and eventually, we walked one last stretch of the park, up to our street, and made it home. One of us knocked on the front door with our knees to announce our arrival. And when it was opened, we stepped in, and the eight of us would sit and enjoy our ice cream, the stress and tension of the journey lifting with each cooling lick.

On one particular summer day when I was around twelve, I was enjoying one of those rare afternoons when Ma let me out on the street to play with the neighbouring kids. Next thing a black car appeared at the top of our street. And as it approached, I was shocked to see that my Da was driving and parked it right outside our house. I ran over and asked him who owned the car. "It's my car, I bought it from a workmate," he told me proudly with a big smile on his face. I couldn't believe it. The Lees had a car, a magnificent four-door car with black shiny seats. Then Ma, Philomena, and Michael came out, and they were just as surprised as I was.

We all climbed in, and I heard Ma say to Da, " I didn't know you could drive Canice!" "Yes," he replied " I learned at the airport". "But can we afford it, how are we going to pay for it?" she asked. He said it was already paid for from his winnings at the race track. When Ma and Da went into the house, we stayed in the car for at least half an hour. We gazed around, taking in every detail of the interior, and enjoying the fact that we could be seen by all the neighbours. It was soon time to go back into the house, and I discovered my bare legs were stuck to the seat. I had to peel them off slowly to release myself.

Every afternoon that week, whenever Da was home, I spent my time walking around the car beaming with pride. I inspected every inch, the front and back fenders, the bonnet and grill, the doors, handles, and wing mirrors. As neighbours passed by, I was in constant readiness to inform them that this was our car. My mind was filled with the exciting possibilities that this car brought for our family. We could go on trips to the beach, to the country and on visits to our relatives. But my plans for outings were short-lived as it soon became clear that the car was for Da and Da alone.

Before long, I began to resent the car that had once given me such great pride and joy. He no longer let us sit in the backseat, he didn't take us anywhere, so when he was home, it just sat there, parked, blocking the street when my neighbours and

I wanted to play soccer and other games outside. Even when we moved the goalposts farther down the street, we had to be careful not to kick the ball too far to avoid hitting the car and infuriating Da. Ma used to sit at the front room window watching us, and if she heard a bang, we would be unceremoniously dragged into the house for a beating. Worst of all, our friends were made aware of exactly what was facing us once we got inside the door. Even when we weren't out playing ourselves, she was ever ready to rush out to chastise the local kids if they hit the car. I used to hope that Da wouldn't come home early so we could play our games uninterrupted on those lovely sunny days.

A special treat that I will never forget was when our Ma took us on a Mystery Tour. These were organised by the Bus Company on Sundays during the summer. Several buses would leave the city centre on a day-long, roundtrip journey, to a destination which was kept secret from the passengers. The idea was for us to pick a bus and take our chance to see what that journey would reveal. On one particular Mystery Tour, as we drove deeper into the countryside, the scenery became greener and greener. The excitement in the bus was building, by the mile, and the chatter was getting louder. When we finally reached our destination and alighted the bus, we discovered we were in Glendalough (the Glen of Two Lakes) in County Wicklow. Before exiting the bus, the conductor shouted out, "You have to be back here by four o'clock," and that was our cue to set off and explore our destination.

I was amazed by the beauty of this magical place: the woods, lakes, streams and mountains. There was also a tall tower and a very old derelict church. We were free to roam around as we pleased, as long as we were within Ma's sight. The only break we took was for our picnic of sandwiches and a drink which we had sitting together on the grass.

That afternoon we took a boat across one of the lakes. Our tour guide showed us St. Kevin's Bed, a tiny cave cut into the rock on the edge of the mountain about thirty feet above the lake. He explained that St. Kevin had lived here as a hermit around the year 600 and used this cave as his bed and a place for prayer. Michael Dwyer, the famous Wicklow rebel, was reputed to have taken shelter here while on the run from British soldiers during the 1798 Irish rebellion. He escaped capture by diving into the lake and swimming to the opposite side. I knew nothing about this period in our history, and here I was on the very spot where the action took place. I was mesmerised.

The journey home seemed shorter than the trip there. Everyone on the bus was tired but not too tired to join in the singalong led by the bus driver. When we got back to the Quays in Dublin, he lay his cap on the dashboard so the passengers could express their appreciation as they alighted the bus. By the time we

Glendalough in Summer

One of my favourite places in the world

got home to Donnybrook, we were all exhausted after our extraordinary adventure. Glendalough is still one of my favourite places in the world, and I visit it whenever the opportunity arises. It always brings me a sense of peace, perspective, and rejuvenation.

Sandymount Beach, just a thirty-minute walk from home, was another great attraction on those glorious summer days. The tide was usually out when we were there, and the water's edge was out of bounds to us. It was difficult for Ma to sit on the sand without support because of her size. So, to prevent her from falling over, she would ask me to sit with my back to hers. As I sat there with my knees pulled up to my chest, I could feel my heels dig into the sand as she relaxed her weight against me. Thoughts ran through my head that this couldn't be right. *Philomena and Michael were playing, why should I have to do this?* And then the feelings of guilt and atonement slipped in and took over. I was tortured by the fact that everyone had told me I was stupid and worse still, I was evil. Although I didn't understand why this was so, I none the less knew the nuns couldn't be wrong. They had the facts, I was left-handed! And so I did what I was told, without objection. I wanted to be a good boy, I wanted to be loved, but this was not easy, and I struggled inside with the unfairness of it all. This was a struggle I continued to live with throughout my childhood.

When Ma got tired sitting, she would walk over to where a man was selling pots full of boiling water. She would have brought tea leaves to make her own tea, a little bottle of milk, and a cup for herself. While she went about this ritual, it was time for me to get my feet wet, running around in the shallow pools that the tide had left behind as it went out. There was still plenty of time to play, and I made the most of it.

An exceptional treat was a bus ride to Bray. Just over an hour from Dublin, Bray was a vibrant seaside town which in summertime attracted crowds of visitors and the energy and sense of fun along the seafront was exhilarating. Bunting and coloured lights hung from one lamppost to the other. There were bandstands for music and dancing exhibitions, amusement arcades, donkey rides, huckster shops, ice cream and candy floss kiosks, and carnivals with swing boats and chairoplanes. All there to be enjoyed on those long summer days. Sometimes we had a few pennies for the rides or the amusement arcade, but we never asked for chips or ice cream as we knew money was scarce. Ma used to bring treats in her handbag from home, an apple, biscuits, or sweets, and this did us until we got home.

A long promenade stretched from one end of the beach to the other. Ma was terrified something would happen to us if we went into the water, so we were only allowed to splash around on the shore and throw pebbles into the sea. She sat on a bench facing the beach where she could keep an eye on us. Her size meant that she only had limited mobility, but she enjoyed the views and the fresh air. One time, Michael and I asked if we could climb Bray Head and Ma agreed on the condition that we only go partway and then turn back. As we set off on our adventure the excitement was building. We got as far as the chair lifts, which took climbers to the summit, and were envious watching the people getting on and off. Engrossed in all that was going on around us, we lost track of time, and when we got back found Ma in tears. "Ma, what's wrong?" we asked in unison. "I thought you were lost," she said with tears in her eyes. We tried to comfort her and felt sorry that we had made her cry. "Oh Ma," I said, putting my arm around her shoulder. "Come on, Ma, don't be crying," I pleaded. It was hard to see her so upset. We had seen Ma cry before when she was in, what she called, one of her "dark moods". She usually fobbed us off at these times, and we knew not to bother her. This time was different. I sensed a hint of love from her, and I latched on to this.

There was one place where Ma's mood was guaranteed to lighten up, and we'd see a side of her, we never got to experience the rest of the year. This was on our visits to her home in Cloghore, Donegal, the highlight of our summer holidays. Visiting our grandparents in Cloghore not only filled us with joy but also gave Ma two weeks of relief when she was in top form.

In turn, this gifted us with two weeks of no fear-inducing broom knocking on the ceiling, and of no one bursting into our room to beat us for being too loud. Two weeks when we could go to bed at a reasonable time and experience the lives of other kids. Two weeks of bliss in my world.

My grandparents, aunts and uncles, always hoped that Da would join us on holidays, but he never did. They had only known the side of him that was charming and entertaining and would have welcomed him with open arms. Ma gave the excuse of it being a busy time of the year for him at the airport. In reality, he had no desire to spend time in their company. In the end, it worked out for the best because we could all relax in his absence, even Ma.

To reach our destination, we had a long and tortuous journey ahead of us, with our cases and bags of gifts in hand. It started with a bus trip from Donnybrook to Connolly Train Station in Dublin City, followed by the three-hour train ride. During one of these trips, when I was around seven, my mother sat me in the corner near the window and almost completely covered me with her large arm, to hide me from the conductor as she hadn't paid for me. I was told to keep quiet and not move. When the tickets were being checked, l could see the conductor looking over behind my mother. I held my breath in shock as our eyes met, but he said nothing. Every time he walked through our carriage, I was terrified he would throw me off the train, alone, in the middle of nowhere, so I sat rigid in the corner for the entire three hours, while Philomena and Michael were free to play and run up and down the train car until we arrived at Sligo. I can only assume that the conductor knew we were poor and decided to overlook the matter. Why me? Well, Michael was already travelling free, because of his age, and Ma chose me over Philomena because she knew I would obey. Philomena, on the other hand, would go hysterical if asked to do something she didn't want to do.

The next stage of our journey was a one-and-a-half-hour bus ride to Ballyshannon. En route we travelled through what I was later to learn was Yeats's country. The sight of Benbulbin was the first real sign that we were almost there. Once we hit Finner Camp, an Irish army barracks originally built by the British, we knew we were just minutes away from our destination, and the excitement began to brew within us. The last short leg of our journey was in a taxi, owned by a neighbour of our grandparents who picked us up at the bus stop. When we arrived, Granny and Granda were always standing outside the house waiting to greet us. Everyone embraced, and we were all happy, especially Ma. She was home in her familiar and beloved countryside, surrounded by family and friends, in complete contrast to the isolation she had chosen to maintain in Dublin.

Granny was a tiny woman no more than five feet tall and very slight in build. She had tight curly hair and wore black-rimmed glasses. In the house, she had a special seat against the wall facing the cooking range where she had full view of the living room. From here, she conducted proceedings while smoking her Woodbine cigarettes with a distinctive drag and smack sound as she pulled it from her puckered lips. She warned us of the dangers of smoking but didn't seem to be able to give up the habit herself. Meanwhile, Granda sat in a chair to the side of the range where he smoked his pipe. Beside him on the floor was a spittoon into which he spit phlegm intermittently. I always felt this was a disgusting habit, but it didn't put me off my granddad because I loved him dearly. He was a tall, thin, pleasant man with silver hair and a moustache. During his time working for the council, he was part of the team who built the local road up the side of the hill, which could be clearly seen from the house. He took great pride in showing us this road every time he took us for walks around the countryside, and we used to call it Granddad's road. One day he took us to a pond and grabbed two stones from the water, cracked them together and made a spark. This was impressive, a skill worth acquiring, and Michael and I practised all evening until, with great satisfaction, we mastered it.

Our grandparent's house was a small three-bedroom semidetached council bungalow, one of ten such houses set among acres of open fields begging to be explored. There was no running water or indoor bathroom facilities. Rainwater, collected in a barrel outside of the house, was used to wash, and the drinking water had to be collected in buckets from the well up the road. There was a toilet in an outside shed comprising of a very large metal bucket with a handle and an ill-fitted, plastic toilet seat. Every two to three days, Granda would go up to the backfield, dig a hole and empty it. The smell in the shed was horrific. We used to hold our breath as long as possible and could often be seen rushing out, gasping for air, to the amusement of any onlookers who were used to this, and saw us as weak city folk. Since I was in no hurry to experience this dreadful stench, I would try to time my visits to coincide with Granda returning from the field with an empty and cleaned container. The pungent smell of disinfectant was most definitely the lesser of two evils. It certainly made us appreciate our flush toilet at home, albeit outdoors.

In the garden, my grandparents kept chickens and a cow called Moggy. They also had a black-and-white dog, Toby, that was very playful and frightened us at first because we weren't used to dogs. Every morning Granda would take Moggy out from her pen, walk her down by the side of the house and up to a neighbour's field to graze. They allowed him to do this in return for grass cutting and odd jobs. Many mornings, I would eagerly ask Granda if I could come, to which he'd respond with a resounding, "Yeah, of course!" He never denied me an outing with him. I'd stay close to his side as we walked off and observed all his orders. At the end of the day, Moggy would be taken back home and milked. The warm milk being squeezed into a metal bucket was an extraordinary sight for us, city kids. I never liked the strong taste of this warm milk, it seemed to linger on my tongue, but it was our only option, so I had no choice in the matter.

Later in the afternoon, I'd go down to the well with Granda to fill buckets with drinking water and bring them back up to the house. When I proudly carried one all on my own, my Granda would look down and say, "Hey Patrick, you're doing a great job there, you're spilling very little," and my chest would swell with pride. So I offered to fetch water every day, and he happily agreed. I became proficient at collecting it without spilling any on the way home, and every time I returned with the two buckets still full, he was so delighted, he'd say, "By God, isn't he a great cub!" To which even my mother, who never offered any compliments at home, would suddenly say, "Ah, yeah". I was delighted they were happy with me and this felt good.

Granny allowed us to play up and down the road, and if there was any form of protest from Ma, she'd say encouragingly,

Me proudly delivering my two buckets of water 1961

"Let the wee cubs go. They'll be fine." And that was our green light. Ma enjoyed this, too, because that meant she had some alone time in the kitchen with her mother and sister, who lived with her family next door. Funnily enough, whereas we led a sheltered existence in Dublin, here in Cloghore, we were considered adventurous city slickers. Our visits were a great novelty for the local children who joined us as we explored the surrounding fields and byways and quizzed us about the goings-on in the "big bad city". We only discovered afterwards that some of the places we went were out of bounds to them, and they used us as an excuse to get some freedom.

On one of our adventures, we were playing in a field when, out of the blue, a bull started chasing us. I saw a small fence which I knew I could clear, so headed straight toward it. I leapt up in the air, not knowing that on the other side I would meet a seven-foot drop straight into a mess of cow shit. The others were breaking their hearts in laughter, rolling around on the grass, as I climbed out covered in crap. We knew we'd all be in trouble if the grown-ups saw me in that state. So we had to devise a plan to get to the well, without being seen. We decided to lie on our bellies and crawl past the houses like commandos until we were safe. When we got to the well, I knelt down on my hands and knees, and they vigorously pumped the water over me until the shit streamed down my clothes and body. By the time I got back to Granny and Granda's my clothes were dry and it looked like we had managed to avert getting into trouble.

Unfortunately for us, somebody eventually squealed, and Ma was furious. Assuming we had been leading the neighbours' kids astray, she made us pay for letting her down and "making a show" of her. We were taken us up to an isolated bog road close to the house, and as soon as we were out of sight, she whipped us across the legs with a switch (a very small branch). This felt like a sharp nettle sting, but we took our punishment, dried our tears and walked back to the house, acting as if all was well. We were just happy that this was the end of the matter, and we were back in our grandparents' home.

Occasionally, we were taken on trips to nearby Bundoran, a typical seaside town. On Sundays, an auctioneer came selling all kinds of bric-a-brac. He mesmerised his audience, offering unbeatable deals, and I had to be dragged away from his stand. It seemed as if he could sell anything and I longed for the day when I could come back to Bundoran with money in my pockets. I would then be able to enjoy the fun palaces, the rides, buy chips along the seafront, and take advantage of all the auctioneer's fabulous bargains.

One summer I actually did have a little money but didn't get the opportunity to enjoy it. That year just before we left for our holidays, my brother Michael and I ran into Uncle Michael in

Donnybrook Village. He was working as a delivery man for beers and soft drinks and, when we told him we were off to Donegal, he said "I'll be down near your Granny's next week making a delivery. If I see you, I'll give you a few free Fizzy drinks." We couldn't resist his offer, so the following week we made the long walk into Ballyshannon and waited outside Mulligan's pub as instructed. When he eventually came, he gave us each our bottle of pop. Then, after some brief small talk, asked, "Do you have any money on you?" I proudly showed him what I had, seven shillings and sixpence, all my holiday money saved money saved over a year in the children's Penny Bank behind Donnybrook Church. "Can I borrow that for a few minutes? I'll bring it straight back to you." I hesitated and reluctantly handed it over. That is the last we saw of him, his lorry or my money. I was shocked and furious "He's gone Michael," I said. "He robbed me, a full year's savings! How could he do it to me? My uncle?" There were no answers and nothing we could do but start walking home.

As we approached the house, we could see Ma, Granny, and Auntie Rosaleen on the road. They had been worried sick and were out searching for us. Relief washed over their faces when they spotted us. When I finally explained what had happened, they weren't a bit surprised. Uncle Michael was a known gambler, I guess it ran in the Lee family, so they knew he had swindled me.

Granny, Rita, Philomena, Michael and myself 1957

The only photo I have with Granda 1958

He had probably bet on a "sure thing" in the nearby betting shop and scampered as soon as he lost. I could see they were sorry for me but not sorry enough to make up any of my losses. This was the first time I was directly affected by gambling, the curse of our family, and the sting was sharp and painful.

Belleek, a town in Northern Ireland just over the border from Cloghore, held a particular attraction for me. It had one of the widest streets I had ever seen with shops on either side. At one end was a fabulous hotel on the banks of the Erne, and at the other end, on the hill, stood a church. We visited here about twice a week to buy English sweets and more importantly, to attend Market Day. This was spectacular and attracted lots of business to the town. Stalls were set up all along the main street selling everything imaginable including vegetables, fruit, horses, cattle, and sheep. The pub doors were open, and the men took their pints out onto the street. The animals were led there by their tough-looking owners in big topcoats and "pee-pee" caps. Most had either a cigarette or pipe in one hand and a stick in the other to control their animals.

It was a fabulous and fascinatingly different world for me. To watch them negotiate a sale, was a true revelation. They would propose a price with a spit on their hands and, if accepted, shake on it to seal the deal. Cash was then counted and exchanged for the animal, which was led away by its new owner. Somehow this made me feel sad as I thought of the poor animal having to leave his home and move to unfamiliar surroundings. Each farmer had their own unique negotiating style, and always consciously played to the crowd. I marvelled at the entire deal-making process as I walked unaccompanied from group to group. When my Granda called me to go home, I would ask him to let me stay a little longer. I couldn't get enough of this excitement, and he saw it and gave me an extra ten minutes to soak it all in. On the walk home, we held hands and chatted incessantly, me asking questions, and him explaining with joy and pride about the workings of the marketplace. My passion for trading was truly ignited on that street.

Once, after returning from one of these market days, I remember walking into the house famished only to see a big pot of cabbage and potatoes. Then my Granny said to my Granda, "Will you get a chicken?" He readily agreed and went out to the yard and over to the pen, with me following close behind. The next thing I knew, he was in the pen, catching an actual live chicken, putting it under his arm and, in one swift move, cracking the bird's neck. Then he looked up to see me, handed me the dead chicken, and said, "There you are, pluck as much of that as you can." I dutifully found a spot and plucked away, then handed it back to Granda, who got right to work, chopping the neck off and removing the innards. Then he placed the chicken into a bin full of rainwater that had been collected from the gutters, carefully washed it and brought the chicken into my Granny, who quickly seasoned it and put it in the oven. In less than two hours, we sat at the table and were served a beautiful piece of fresh, hot chicken, with flowery potatoes still in their skins and glistening with butter. Mouthwatering and absolutely delicious.

There was one particular day I spent with Granda which I will never forget. I was about twelve, and it was one of the last of those spectacular summer holidays in Donegal. That morning, we set out down to a neighbour's field, and I watched him cut the grass with a large scythe. I was fascinated by his tall, skinny, frame as it moved from side to side, cutting through the tall blades with each swing of the scythe. All the while he'd say, "You've got to be careful using this, you could cut your leg off!" As I stood there keenly observing him, the postman came by and shouted across to Granda that there was mail for him. "I'll walk up with you to the house," said Granda, then turned to me and said he'd be back in a while.

After watching them disappear up the road, I sat in the field waiting for him. As the minutes ticked by it dawned on me that he'd probably decided to stay for a while and have a cup of tea, have a smoke and listen to the women chatting, so I decided to have a go at using the scythe myself. I picked it up, felt its weight in my hands, and got started. I was in awe at how, with one movement, swoosh, the tall blades of grass fell like angels on the ground. It was so beautiful and graceful that I was mesmerised by the experience. Suddenly, I found my rhythm and swing, and before I knew it, I had cut the entire field. By the time Granda got back, I was just sitting on the wall waiting for him, and he was utterly amazed at what I had done. For the following three days, he told everyone and anyone, "Did you see the field? The wee cub cut it!" He also made sure to tell Ma, "Maura, I'll tell ya one thing, that lad will never be short of work." I felt truly appreciated and was over the moon with pride and joy.

On the last day of our holidays, I was always upset, crying because I didn't want to leave these two people who showered me with so much love and kindness. I first embraced Granny, my arms tight around her waist, as I told her how much I loved her. And then came Granda who also allowed me to hug him. "We'll see you again. It won't be long before you are back." he'd say. I soaked in that last bit of comfort and love in hopes that it would last me until the following summer visit. I had been named after my Granda, but this wasn't the only thing we had in common. We were both hard workers, and I felt there was a unique bond between us. Without knowing it, he built up my confidence like no other and gave me the strength to pursue my dreams.

From the moment we stepped on the train back to Dublin, Ma's happiness visibly dissipated before our eyes. Suddenly,

Donegal began to feel like it was a million miles away with only potatoes and carrots, that Granda had pulled fresh from the ground, to remind us of our days with them. As far as Ma was concerned that bag of vegetables extended the holiday experience, which only officially ended when all our Donegal stocks had been eaten. Potatoes and rhubarb were stretched out for as many days as possible. Once washed and put on to boil, we would wait eagerly for the potatoes, Ma testing occasionally with a knife to see if they were cooked through. As they emerged from the pot, the skins would start to fall away to reveal what looked like white puffy balls of flour. Butter was generously spread across the plate of potatoes, and we would watch as it melted in golden streams running down the sides. There was nothing nicer, no need for meat or other vegetables. These potatoes, skins and all, laced with butter were a delicious treat just on their own. When we had to revert to local Dublin potatoes, Ma would complain sardonically about their lack of taste and texture. We didn't see that much difference ourselves, but we knew what she was really saying: she missed Cloghore.

Chapter 6

New Horizons

When I was about twelve, one of our elderly neighbours asked me to go shopping for her on Saturday mornings, and for this, she gave me a few pennies. Word got around, and within weeks I was doing the same for other elderly neighbours. Everyone on my street was aware that if they couldn't get out to do their own shopping, I could be called on. It was great to be trusted and to have the opportunity to help. The tips were not bad, either.

Each of the women I shopped for gave me a list of what they needed. Since I had difficulty reading, I would hand this list over to the various shopkeepers. Groceries were bought from Martin's or Stein's; these were the grocery stores where the best value was to be had—the Corner House was too expensive, so I avoided this one. All fruit and vegetables could be bought from Christy's horse and cart, and for meats, I went to Fields Butchers. From the outside of Fields, the full range of what was available could be seen through large glass windows. Laid out in steel trays were steaks, mincemeat, rashers, and liver. Hanging from the ceiling on large hooks were strings of sausages, black and white puddings, chickens, rabbits, large joints of meat, and even half a pig. The floor was covered with sawdust and customers carried it out on their feet, creating a trail outside on the path. The butcher's apron was always spotted with blood. And around his waist was a leather belt with a wooden holder from which all his knives hung. For a young boy, it was an awesome sight.

Shortly after I started shopping for my neighbours, Christy offered me a Saturday job on his horse and cart, helping him serve his customers. I couldn't believe my luck! I accepted in a blink of an eye before he had even told me the pay. The thought of riding on this cart around Donnybrook would have been reward enough, but Christy gave me five shillings for the day's work. Amazing! What's more, I still managed to get the shopping done for my neighbours before he arrived at the top of our street, his first stop of the day.

Christy catered to about seven hundred families living in council housing in the area. As well as Home Villas we called to Pembroke cottages, Beaver Row, and Beech Hill. The cart travelled around the streets, stopping at the same points every week, where it could be clearly seen by the surrounding houses. Extra stocks were delivered by a van to two of Christy's stopping points to replenish the goods on the cart. One of these was at the

Cottages and the other at the top of our hill. The large sacks were lined up on the street ready to be placed on the cart, as space became available. When I had shopped for fruit and vegetables for my neighbours, before I worked for Christy, I often gave him a hand to lift the heavy sacks of potatoes onto the cart from the path. This is actually how he first got to know me.

Customers would come in two's and three's, and if any of them were short of cash on the day, they would get their goods "on tick" until the following week. For some families, this became an ongoing scenario where the previous week's goods were paid for, and the current week's went on tick again. Christy kept a book with all the details, but he never made people feel bad because they didn't have money on the day, he never doubted that he would get paid.

For the early part of the day, I would sit on the back of the cart with my legs dangling down, watching the road disappear beneath my feet. Once the stocks depleted sufficiently, I could move and sit up front with Christy. As we trotted along the streets, you could hear the clip-clap of the horse's hooves on the road. On sunny days, I relished the glorious heat on my back and the sight of the glistening windows as we passed by the houses. In the rain, I was invigorated by the drops rolling down my cheeks, as I watched the streets and houses getting a wash down. Hail, rain, or snow, it did not matter to me. I felt like a cowboy, raised above the everyday goings-on, other children looking up at me in envy. At every stop, I hopped down to help weigh the vegetables and fill the shopping bags for the customers. Sometimes I had to call to the houses if people were slow to come to the cart. This was where I got my first experience of cold calling and rejection. I soon learned this was all part of the process, and not to be taken personally—a lesson I would carry with me well into the future and my career as an adult. Christy would often ask me to carry a customer's bag to their house if it was heavy and I always got a few pennies for this. These I would put in my pockets which had holes in them, so I'd feel the money trickle down my legs and into my smelly but sturdy wellington boots.

We were treated with great kindness by the customers on our route who brought us cups of tea and sometimes biscuits out to the cart. Christy would always have a Sweet Afton cigarette with his. The tea was like nectar, and whatever I had to eat, a biscuit or a piece of fruit from the cart tasted delicious to me. Hunger is a great sauce! If it was pouring rain, the neighbours might even invite us into their homes to shelter. Just like Ma did during that first frightful storm I remember so vividly from when we lived at 25 Home Villas.

I met a lot of interesting people during my days working for Christy. Among them was Fred Tiedt who had won a silver medal in boxing at the Melbourne Olympics in 1956. I was only

Home Villas

seven at the time, but I can remember it vividly. Word on the ground was that he was robbed of the gold, but we were hugely proud of the silver medal—this was something to be celebrated. At the gates of Herbert Park, just twenty feet from his home and fifty feet from mine, we had an enormous bonfire. Neighbours brought out old furniture and any combustible rubbish they had and piled it on the fire, which stood about fourteen feet high. It was a magnificent sight. We all chanted "We want Fred, we want Fred" and when the door finally opened, and he appeared, the crowd went wild. We had a hero in our midst, and that made us incredibly proud. To meet him later on my vegetable route, and get the chance to shake his hand, was a real privilege.

I have many treasured memories of my time on the horse and cart. Not least of these is that last fifteen-minute journey home from Beech Hill to Donnybrook when our day was done. The only weight on the cart was Christy and me, so the horse travelled with speed. The road was ours, and the world was mine. It was exhilarating. When the horse and cart finally came to a stop, Christy put his hand deep into his leather bag and pulled out two half-crowns for me. I jumped down from the cart, and it was only when my feet touched the ground that I realised how tired I was. But it was a good tired, a satisfying feeling after a great day's work.

As I walked down the street to my house, I could feel the coins jingle in my wellington boots. And when I got home, nothing gave me greater joy than handing them over to Ma filled with money. She would empty them into a basin filled with hot water to wash the precious coins that had been harboured in my stinking boots all day. Then she carefully counted the money on the dining table, setting aside the pennies and halfpennies to give to me. I got the copper, she kept the silver. It never dawned on me to look for more. The first time this transaction occurred, and she brought a basin filled with hot water, I joyfully assumed it was for me to soak my smelly feet after a hard day's work. I couldn't believe she was being so thoughtful and was thrilled until she started placing the coins in the basin instead of my feet. I had to walk up and down in the back garden, wiping my bare feet on the grass to freshen them. Ma always worried about where the weekly rent would come from and inadvertently transferred this worry to me. I was just happy that she now had enough money to pay the pound-a week rent.

My life truly started to have a value with that little job on the horse and cart. For the first time in my life, I had a sense of pride and without knowing it was taking the first steps in choosing a path for my life. The money I earned was never important to me, though it was quite substantial. When the two half-crowns were combined with my tips, I never got less than a pound and three shillings for the day. Furthermore, it was my first experience receiving gratitude and compliments from strangers. This was confirmation of what my Granda believed, that I was capable of doing something with my life.

Now I was doing something I was good at, and loved every minute of it. Saturday was the best day of the week. To top it off, the delight in Ma's eyes, and her change in attitude toward me—especially as Saturday drew nearer—was an immense relief. And by Sunday she was off my back. Even though she reverted to her usual scowling self on Monday, my life at home was generally better. I was now attempting to buy her love, fully aware of how important money was to her. This would become the pattern of our relationship and would eventually lead me to steal for her. Love was never forthcoming, but as long as I could keep the money flowing, I was of value to her, and life was bearable.

It was around this time that I took up smoking .... paper! I would roll up strips of newspaper in the form a cigarette, light up, and suck on it as if I was smoking a cigarette. It didn't taste good and made me light-headed, but it did make me feel so grown up, just like the guys in the movies. The only place I felt safe to do this was in our outside toilet. There were plenty of newspaper pieces here, hanging on a string, as we used them for toilet paper. My only concern was that the next person in the toilet would smell the smoke, and I would get into trouble with Ma. So each time I took a drag from the "cigarette," I blew the smoke out through one of the three ventilation holes on the door. What I did not realise was that I was sending out clear smoke signals, broadcasting to the world that I was smoking. What an ass! I am sure this did not go unnoticed by my neighbours, but no one reported it to Ma, so I never got caught. In time, I would move on to real cigarettes, which were much more enjoyable.

Within that same year, I was lucky enough to get a second job on Sunday mornings as Milkman Larry's assistant. His was a smaller, more high-quality cart than Christy's. It had a footstep to help you get on and a comfortable bench seat for the driver and his assistant. Larry was very proud of his copper milk churns which stood about four feet tall on the back of the cart. He kept them in pristine condition, polishing them continuously. This job paid three sixpenny pieces, and my duties were to knock on doors to let people know that the milkman was outside. When customers did not want to come out of their houses to get their own milk, I would bring their jugs to be filled for them. Apart from the money I earned, this job gave me another opportunity to ride on a horse and cart. To my thirteen-year-old self, this was absolutely fantastic. An even bigger bonus was that Ma allowed me to go to the pictures on my own on Sunday afternoons, now that I had the extra money. I was over the moon as films were my everything.

My love affair with films had started a few years earlier when Da took us to the cinema for the first time. I was instantly enthralled by the whole spectacle, and it spearheaded what was to become a lifelong passion for film. I loved cowboy movies, which fed my very active imagination and formed the basis of my newfound dream world, my go-to escape from reality at home. When I went to bed at night, I would burrow down below my pillow alongside the "bolster" pillow separating me from Michael. I'd pull the blankets up over my head, leaving just a small slit to look out through, creating my very own dreamland. Here I could be a cowboy on a horse upon a mountain looking down on the Indians, or Tarzan swinging from branch to branch. These imaginary adventures allowed me to drift happily off to sleep without a care in the world.

The picture house I frequented as a teenager was the Sandford in Ranelagh. On Saturday and Sunday afternoons they had what was called the "the sixpenny rush," and as I was working all day Saturday, Sunday was my day for the pictures. These weekly outings further fuelled my passion for movies. The show would start at two-thirty, so I'd leave the house at about one forty-five to take the twenty-minute walk up to Ranelagh. I wanted to get there early to be first in the queue so I could choose my favourite seat. Right beside the picture house, was the candy shop, an Aladdin's cave of all things sweet in huge jars with screw-top lids. These would have to be weighed out and put into small white bags, which were sealed with a twist of the wrist. It was here I got my gobstoppers, bullseyes, and fizz pops, all the sweets I wasn't given as a young child. I would place my purchases in my pocket and wait until I was in the cinema before starting to eat them. As two-thirty approached, the queue of mostly children would stretch right around the corner. When the man came to open the big gates of the picture house, the excitement was palpable. The gates folded back like a melodeon and I took the four steps up into the main building and to the ticket kiosk.

Once my ticket was checked, an usher would lead me into the dark picture house, pointing a flashlight, down the aisle and across the rows of seats. I always went for what to me was the best seat. This was halfway down the cinema against the wall where there was no seat in front to block the view. Here I was also guaranteed not to be disturbed by passersby on their way to the toilet or the shop. This became my regular seat and, after a few weeks, I could have found it blindfolded. When I had a bit more money, I could afford to go up on the balcony, where I would sit in the front row, with a panoramic view of all that was going on downstairs. The velvet-covered balcony rail provided an excellent place to line up my sweets for the movie. There were ornate light fittings along the walls, which were kept permanently dimmed, and ashtrays attached to the back of every seat. Once seated, I watched all the other children come in and take their places. I kept looking back to the projection room, for the operator to come. Finally, the waiting was over. The dimmed lights went out, and the heavy red velvet curtains opened to reveal a large screen. Next thing, a shell appeared and opened, and the words Pearl and Dean appeared. This signalled the start of the advertisements, and even these gripped my attention.

Soon the first film would start and reality suspended as we entered the imaginary world of movies. This was what was called a "Follier-upper," which was in black-and-white and lasted about forty minutes, leaving us in eager anticipation until the following week. And then, the feature film began in full technicolour. The movies we saw were all the blockbusters of the day: The Loneliness of the Long Distance Runner; Ben Hur; The 10 Commandments; White Lightning; It's a Wonderful Life; The OK Corral; The Lone Ranger and Tonto; and High Noon. I loved the ones that featured Gary Cooper or Henry Fonda. They always played quiet, strong men with a sense of justice. I looked up to them because this was the kind of man I wanted to become. Before I knew it, the film was over, and the National Anthem was playing. Out we poured into the street struggling to adjust our eyes to the daylight. I couldn't wait for the following Sunday. When I went to bed that night, I would be transported back to the picture house and revisit the entire program in my mind. Magic, pure magic.

The pictures provided me with an insight into a world I knew nothing about and escapism from the reality of my life. I now had a wealth of material with which to create a vision of the life I wanted for myself. Films demonstrated how important it was to have respect, loyalty, and integrity, good examples of which were missing from my home life. I was inspired to cultivate a strong moral code. I believed that everything was possible, but this was not consistent with what my family had in mind for me. There was consternation and ridicule when I voiced my ambitions, so I learned to keep them to myself. However, the foundations were laid, and the ideas firmly imprinted on my mind.

Chapter 7

Catholic Puberty

As a frightened, insecure boy, I found great peace and strength in prayer, and I think my belief in God helped keep me sane. One day I was feeling particularly happy with God and wanted to do something to let him know I was grateful. There was a statue of him towering on a pedestal in the church grounds, and I stretched up on my tiptoes and placed a sixpence coin, all the money I had in the world, at his feet. I felt good and proud of myself as I walked home from the church. A week later, I went back to check that he had taken it, and to my surprise, it was still there. I concluded that he didn't want or need it, so I took it back. It was just enough to go to the pictures. Oh happy days, thank you, God!

We'd go to church every Sunday for Mass, all of us except for Ma who only went when she was home in Donegal with her family. Back in Dublin, while she didn't join us, she cared so much about the optics that she always made sure we didn't miss it. Even though Da was a believer, we never said prayers in the house as a family. No grace before meals, no goodnight prayers, so our religion came from school and these weekly masses. Whenever Da was around on Sundays, he went to Donnybrook Church with his pocket-size prayer book and rosary beads. He always wore his Trilby hat, gently tipping it to greet any neighbours who walked by. He used to say to us, "You go on, and I'll catch up to you," but he never did. He'd walk all the way to church on the opposite side of the road not only avoiding us but all our neighbours, not wanting to get into a conversation.

As I grew a little older, I had to figure out life one day at a time. To survive, I learned to hide my pain and loneliness. My belief in God helped carry me through the hellish times at home and school. But, in time, my anxiety began to take its toll on me. I retreated deeper into myself, surviving only by going into my imaginary world in my little safe haven in bed. I used to distract myself dreaming about cowboy films until I fell asleep. By the time I was eleven, that imaginary world was no longer helpful. That's when I started the habit of rolling from side to side in bed, what my family called jockeying. My mind was blank, but my body couldn't stop moving. It was like rocking myself to sleep, calming myself from the mental and emotional stress I was under until I finally let go and entered the world of rest.

Disturbed by the creaking sound of the bed, my siblings would call down to Ma "Patrick is jockeying again, we can't get to sleep". Ma would beat me, but nothing she did could stop me. When we were in Donegal on holidays, she told me that she and Auntie Rosaleen were going to take me to see a Monk in nearby Rossnowlagh. He had the gift of healing and would be able to sort out my "unnatural" jockeying. It didn't matter that I vehemently objected, I was going, and that was that. Everyone in Granny's house seemed to know about my problem. I felt humiliated and victimised again, but this time it was in full view of my family, which was unbearable.

When we got to the monastery, we were greeted by a Monk who appeared to be expecting us. He was dressed in a long brown robe with a rope tied around the waist, open sandals on his bare feet and a large crucifix hung around his neck. All this made him look very holy and authoritative. He brought me into a small cubicle leaving Ma and Aunt Rosaleen outside. I was terrified, my stomach was in turmoil, and I felt as if I was going to vomit. The monk put his hands on my head and began to pray. He told me that jockeying was the devil's work and that God would be very disappointed in me if I didn't stop. *What? More evil?* I thought and began to cry. When he saw how upset I was, he said " I don't think you are a bad boy, but you have to stop this jockeying. Can you do this for God, can you promise God today that you will stop?" "yes, I will," I replied. He then gave me a special blessing that would help me and laid his hands on my head again. We returned to Ma and my aunt Rosaleen, and he triumphantly reported that I was cured. They thanked him, and as we left, I noticed my aunt hand him an envelope, presumably a donation. I went to bed that evening and did not jockey, terrified that I might break my promise. I had great difficulty getting to sleep, and this continued for many nights. I never jockeyed again but missed the comfort it brought. Leaving Donegal that summer, everyone was delighted with me and proud that their Donegal healer had been the one to cure me.

About a year later, I came home one day to find Ma in a flood of tears. "Your Granda is dead," she cried repeatedly. "We have to go home, I need to be there." A deep sadness came over me, and I kept to myself throughout the long journey to Cloghore to attend his wake. I had no experience with death and didn't know what was ahead of me. As we approached my grandparent's house, I could see cars parked everywhere and the house itself was full of people who had come to pay their respects. They had brought loads of food and drink, enough to last for weeks.

Ma, as the oldest daughter, busied herself looking after the mourners and seemed to be in her element taking care of things. Granda was laid out in the bedroom with the chief mourners standing around the room. People filed in, in an orderly queue, to see him and touch his hands for one last time before the coffin was closed. Everyone was shaking hands and talking about what a great man he was. My sister, Philomena, was encouraged to go into the room to see Granda, and when she said no, Ma tried to pull her in. Philomena dug her heels into the ground and wouldn't move. "I don't want to go in, I don't want to see him" she cried hysterically and got her way.

When it was my turn to say goodbye, touching his hands wasn't enough for me. I instinctively got up on my tiptoes, leaned over the edge of the coffin and kissed him. As my lips touched his forehead, it felt like kissing a block of ice, I was shocked, my Granda was gone. I stepped back, in a flood of tears, devastated. I knew he loved and believed in me. And that belief would eventually carry me far from the confines of 6 Home Villas, further than he or I, could ever have imagined.

Meanwhile, anxiety continued to be an issue for me, and I turned to food for comfort. That's when I began to put on a lot of weight and acquired the nickname Poncho Lee at school. People were quick to let me know I was getting fat as if I was not already aware. But the food was now my crutch. Out of frustration with the constant jeering and abuse, and having no possibility of defending myself openly, I developed a coping mechanism of cursing my persecutors under my breath. I'd silently curse my teacher, "You think you're so great, you haven't a fucking clue, you baldy headed fecker. When I'm a man, I'll come back, in an even bigger car than yours and wads of money in my pocket. I'll show you how feckin' wrong you were, you first-class bollocks." I'd even curse Ma behind her back, "Who the feck do you think you're talking to? I fucking hate you." This cursing was incredibly therapeutic, and it brought me great relief. The downside of this was the guilt instilled by my Catholic upbringing. This left me in fear of being condemned to the fires of hell. Saturday confessions, when I could have my soul cleansed, couldn't come soon enough. It was a very stressful week if I happened to commit a mortal sin on a Monday, hoping to God that I wouldn't die before I got to confess.

As if all that weren't enough, puberty came knocking on my door and caught me completely by surprise. When I woke up one morning and experienced what I would later realise was my first erection, I thought there was something wrong with me, so I told no one. I feared that this was another manifestation of evil in me, just like my left hand and my jockeying. I had no wish to bring on another visit to Rossnowlagh, to have the monk give me a blessing, especially not down there! I hadn't been given the "birds and the bees" talk and had no one I could trust to ask about what was happening to me. I became so stressed about this latest evil that my erection solved itself. Everything finally made sense when, sometime later, a priest came to our school to explain the facts of life. Most of my class were two years younger than me and probably only entering this phase. They laughed and jeered as the priest explained what was happening to our bodies, but not me. I was just grateful to learn that there was nothing evil about me or what I was going through, it was was perfectly natural. I left that class a happy and relieved teenager.

Around the same time, I received an invitation to join the altar boys at Donnybrook Church, which was considered a great honour in those days. With this role came a lot of responsibilities and expectations, including being well-behaved and polite at all times. This was a tall order for young boys, but I saw this as an opportunity to get closer to God with the added bonus of socialising.

We were required to be at church thirty minutes before each service, wearing our best clothes and shoes. Once there, we would put on our altar boy robes. These consisted of a black cassock and a white surplice with lace trimmings around the wide sleeves. There were very strict instructions on how to behave when serving mass on the altar. The miracle of transubstantiation was about to happen, and we had to display the utmost respect at this moment. Bread and water would be consecrated and turned into the body and blood of our Lord Jesus Christ. This was a solemn act, and I was only a few feet away witnessing it all. I was in awe. We had to stand with our hands together, fingers straight up to the heavens in a prayer-like fashion, or sit on the altar steps with our hands resting on our knees. Fidgeting or smiling was strictly forbidden. One of the most important things to be done during each ceremony was to recite, in Latin, the responses to the priest's prayers. I can still recall at will full sentences like, *"Quia tu es Deus, fortitude mea: quare me repulisti, et quare tristis incedo, dum affigit me inimicus?"* The words still ring in my ears. Hours were spent teaching us how to correctly pronounce, and put to memory, Latin responses like these. No time at all was given to explaining what these words meant. I never knew what I was rhyming off, and this had nothing to do with not being able to read or write—none of the boys had a clue.

There were some fringe benefits to being an altar boy, such as generous gratuities when serving at baptisms, marriages, and funerals. Also, once a year, the Parish Priests brought us out to a local hotel for a delicious three-course meal, to thank us for our service. The waitresses in the hotel treated us as if we were special and gave us generous portions of everything. After all, we "were growing lads with responsibilities and had to be well fed." It was hard not to feel important. This was confirmed by the fact that altar boys were regularly targeted by religious orders to become priests.

One day, when I was about fifteen, the Parish priest told me that I was one of the chosen few to get an invitation to visit a

Seminary in Leopardstown. Here we'd learn what it would be like to live and train there to be a priest. I had been at school in a different Parish, so the priest had no idea about my reading and writing difficulties, and I wasn't going to enlighten him. So the following Sunday, I headed off proudly to follow my "calling." We joined in with the Community for breakfast and then were shown around the Seminary. When I saw the luxury of the place, everyone with their own bedrooms and a games room, I thought, *This can't be bad, I could live with this!*

After a very tasty lunch, the serious business started. We were told that it was very important for young men like us to answer God's calling to serve him at a higher level. All this sounded very serious and flattering. *They think I have a vocation, wow, maybe I do!* I thought. From my experience, priests were given the utmost respect from everyone and were present at every important community event. Every time a priest visited a house, he was offered cakes and biscuits, and always seemed to be collecting money for the church. This all started to look like a great path to follow until the issue of celibacy came up. "Is there any reason you wouldn't pursue the priesthood?" we were asked. I don't know how I mustered the courage to say, "I want to have my own family." And this brought the discussion, the day, and my short-lived ambition to become a priest, to an abrupt end.

My altar boy days ended soon after, not only because of my increasingly busy schedule, but I began to lose faith in the church. At Mass, I saw money being collected from people who didn't even have enough to support their own families. As I knew well, they couldn't even afford to pay for potatoes from Christy. And here they were under pressure to support the priests who were living in much better conditions than them. It just didn't add up, and in time I came to an understanding that I could separate God from the Church. I decided to avoid all the middlemen, and instead, I developed my own personal relationship with a caring God. This sustained me and brought me through the many difficult years ahead.

Chapter 8

Technical College and the Corner House

My time at St Gaul's National School finally ended with the receipt of a Primary Certificate, which confirmed that I had passed written tests in Irish, English, and Arithmetic. To this day, except for Arithmetic, I have no idea how they could have awarded me this certificate. I assume, at fourteen years of age and two years older than most of my classmates, they couldn't keep me at this school any longer. Maybe it was a going-away present from them to me. Who knows, but as I was clearly not equipped for academia, the only option for further education available to me was technical college, what we called the "tech". The college in Dundrum, a thirty-minute bus ride, was the closest to my home, so this is where I was to spend the next two years.

My Primary Certificate

DEPARTMENT OF EDUCATION
PRIMARY BRANCH

PRIMARY SCHOOL
CERTIFICATE

This is to certify that the pupil named overleaf completed the sixth standard of the programme of instruction in national schools and passed the primary school certificate examination which comprised written tests in Irish, English and Arithmetic, conducted by the Department of Education in June, 1963.

The following are the subjects of the prescribed programme of instruction for the sixth standard in national schools:—

Obligatory Subjects: IRISH, ENGLISH, MATHEMATICS, HISTORY, GEOGRAPHY, MUSIC, NEEDLEWORK (Girls).

Optional Subjects: DRAWING, PHYSICAL TRAINING, RURAL SCIENCE or NATURE STUDY, COOKERY (Girls), LAUNDRY WORK (Girls) or DOMESTIC ECONOMY (Girls), MANUAL INSTRUCTION (Boys).

A going away gift from St Gaul's 1963

While my reading and writing remained a problem, Technical School brought a new set of challenges. This was a more liberal school environment. The bright and quick-witted students became the revered ones of the class, always with an enthusiastic following. Their bravado and one-upmanship showed no mercy to the struggling students whose shortcomings they were happy to exploit as a source of their own entertainment. I was awkward, introverted and lacked confidence because of my academic failings and became one of their regular targets.

Being naturally left-handed, I struggled with the standard technical subjects like metalwork and woodwork. The tools were designed for right-handed people and were very awkward for me to use. I remember one exercise, where I mastered beautifully, the technique of constructing a tongue and groove joint. This is where two pieces of wood are neatly slotted together to become one, without the use of glue or nails. I proudly presented the work to my teacher for inspection only to be completely undermined by his comment, "who did this for you?" I had waited for all my schooldays longing for acceptance. Now, on the one and only occasion when my work was speaking for me, this bastard didn't believe it was mine. Nothing I said would change his mind, how dare he, I was disgusted with him. This moment seemed to encapsulate all my school day experiences. As I stood there being belittled, I could feel my left arm go rigid, and my fist tighten. I imagined my shoulder tipping back, my arm lunging forward and my fist connecting with his jaw. Turning to the class, I raised both my arms high in the air, and everybody clapped and cheered. In reality, I did none of this. My head dropped to my chest, and as I walked back to my work station, I cursed the day I was born.

Whenever I have been asked about my feelings on the abuse and taunting I received, the phrase "It's like water off a duck's back" would roll off my tongue. My immediate reaction was to hide the hurt I felt. In truth, each cruel word penetrated deep into my gut with lasting effects. These were the loneliest two years of my life. As a teenager, I was much more aware of how vicious my peers could be, with their snide comments and innuendos. I never felt so excluded and isolated.

As it turned out, I felt no connection to the trades we were taught at the tech. I was never going to be a carpenter, a mechanic or a plumber. From my job on the horse and cart, I knew I had a knack for dealing with people and wanted to work in sales. When I was fifteen, I had a new chance to pursue what I felt was my calling. My sister Rita came home from work at the Corner House Donnybrook and told me they were looking for a storeroom and yard boy. This could be done after school, all day on Saturdays, and Sunday mornings. Although it meant leaving behind my beloved horse and cart job, I wasn't about to miss this opportunity. This was a high-class grocery store, well known for its wine cellar and cheese counter. The clientele was made up of the nearby rich and famous from the well-to-do Aylesbury, Shrewsbury, and Nutley Roads. The store was owned by Odette Vanockerhout and her German husband, Harry Wilka. Their business was very successful. They lived in a detached house overlooking Killiney Bay, had a holiday home in the Canary Islands and drove an MGB GT sports car. Harry spoke several languages, which was a huge advantage when dealing with customers from the nearby embassies.

I started working at the Corner House shortly after and was given a great variety of tasks to do. I loved every one of them; I swept the floors and the yard, helped carry deliveries from the lorries into the storeroom and packed these away, ready to replenish the shelves as required. Out the back, there was an old oven for burning waste cardboard and packaging, and I kept the place spick and span. The staff behind the various different counters often asked me to help them out, and I gladly did. I learned how to debone ham and to slice smoked salmon. When it was required to take an order on the phone, I'd run over to Rita and ask her in a whisper if she could do it while I fetched the products. She did this willingly, which helped me avoid my whole reading and writing problem. I could not wait to get to work each day. I hurried home from tech, ran to the shop and was always last to leave at 6:30 p.m. Hard work never bothered me and here I had an opportunity to demonstrate this. I loved my job! All the customers knew me and seemed to like me, and I got on very well with my boss and co-workers. Once again, I was valued and appreciated. It felt amazing. Granda would have been so proud of me.

This was so different from the nothingness I was made to feel at home, where I was led to believe that I was worthless and not capable of surviving beyond those walls. I had to bury, deep within, my natural energy and enthusiasm for life. If I voiced an opinion or exhibited any exuberance, I was told to stop being silly and to act my age. All designed to break my spirit and shatter my dreams. I was conditioned from very early on to be subservient and totally dependent on Ma to do my thinking for me. I wish with all my heart that I had known then that one day I would be able to think for myself and break away from her powerful negative influence to claim my own life.

By the time I reached seventeen, my two years at Dundrum Tech were coming to an end. There would be no more mechanical drawing, woodwork, or metalwork. No more time with teachers who didn't inspire me in any way. Those of us who failed our exams had no chance of a job as a tradesman. But I knew there was a full-time job waiting for me at the Corner House, and unlike the rest of the boys who took the summer off before looking for work, I could not wait to get started. It not only meant doing something I was good at and enjoyed but it also that my schooldays, the worst days of my life, were finally over. I was earning better money than with the horse and cart, and little by little, unknown to myself, I was starting to find a smidgen of independence.

Now I was working full-time, I had two half days off during the week to compensate for working at the weekends. This meant I was free to go to the cinema in O'Connell St, the "mecca" for cinema-goers then, and I never missed an opportunity for that. The advantage of going at off-peak times was the avoidance of the very long evening and weekend queues. These could stretch right down the street at peak times and attracted street traders and buskers who provided a distraction while waiting. There was no internet booking then, so if you wanted to be sure to get a seat for a particular movie, you had to go early and get to the front of the queue.

Unlike the multi-screen venues of today, cinemas then had only one screen and often seated as many as a two and a half thousand people. In those days, smoking was permitted, and it seemed as if the majority of cinema-goers smoked. A cloud of smoke was always visible in the stream of light coming from the projection room to the screen. This didn't affect my enjoyment of the movie as I too smoked to my heart's content, consuming a pack of "Silvermints" on my way home to disguise the smell from my breath. Ma sometimes accused me of smoking but, to avoid her wrath, I used to put the smell from my clothes down to the other smoking cinema-goers. Because of the size of the venues, there were several ushers directing people to their seats. They were dressed in smart blazers with silver buttons and carried large torches. There were also girls, dressed in more attractive flimsy outfits, serving ice creams and sweets at the intermission. They would walk down in front of the screen as the lights went on, carrying their heavily laden trays of delights supported by a leather strap around their shoulders.

These afternoons at the cinema were a great treat in the middle of a week. I would carefully consider what movie to see by checking out the advertising materials displayed at each cinema. On one occasion I was particularly impressed by a large cut out of a Roman soldier standing ten feet high outsides the Metropole cinema. With my limited literacy, I jumped to conclusions and thought this was a film, probably like "Ben Hur" and not to be missed. But nothing could have been further from the truth, it was all talking and shouting, and I could not understand most of what they were saying. Worst of all, there were no action scenes like there were in Ben Hur. By the time the film was over, I was seething with anger.

What a fucking waste of time and money, I thought. I certainly wouldn't be recommending this film 'Othello' to anybody.

On the work front, as a full-time employee at the Corner House, I was trained to work in every department and also accompanied the van driver with deliveries to our customers' homes. Most of the houses we visited were enormous, in comparison with Home Villas, and had long wide driveways with expensive cars parked outside. I used to carry the boxes of groceries into the houses and could not believe the size and style of their kitchens. Through huge windows overlooking the back gardens, you could see their well-manicured lawns and flowerbeds. I only realised then how poor we were. Something that struck me at the time was that most of the well to do customers shopped on credit while it was cash-only for the poor. And unlike Christy's less well-off customers, the rich were slower to give tips. But I did not really mind this at the time; I was privy to catching a glimpse of their fabulous houses and seeing how other people beyond Home Villas lived. In bed at night, when I dreamed and planned for my life, I envisioned myself as a millionaire. It was not the money itself I yearned for, but the freedom and lifestyle money could bring. I made a promise to myself then that I would not stop until I found a way to make it. But for now, this would have to wait until after I left 6 Home Villas.

While a whole new horizon had opened up to me in the Corner House, and I loved my job, a dark cloud hung over me all the while I was there. Now that I was working in a shop, Ma started to ask me to steal. As I had become totally dependent on her, I felt I could not refuse. It left me with a terrible feeling in my gut. I was betraying the very people who had given me a lifeline and a sense of worth. I knew it was wrong, and I tried to explain to Ma the enormous risk I was taking, but she would say, "They are only foreigners who've come to this country and are taking our money."

When I tried to make excuses, she ignored me and gave me the silent treatment. Sometimes she would make me feel guilty by saying, "You do whatever you want, never mind about my wants." So there it was, her way or no way - and no way was never an option. The torment of her silence and looks of disdain were worse than the dread of being caught. So I continued to steal whatever she asked for but lived in permanent fear always expecting the worst, to such an extent that it crushed my spirit and made me physically ill. I imagined myself being confronted, fired, having a criminal record, and never being able to work again. I had nightmares about being hauled across the street to the police station. I knew for sure that Ma would not come to my rescue if I was caught and would deny any knowledge or involvement in the crime.

I don't know how aware my siblings were of what I was going through. But it would have been pointless to raise it with them, we did not have the sort relationship that welcomed openness. The illusion of normality in our family would have been shattered, and our toxic environment exposed. Also, Da was not someone I could raise the subject with, if he had found out what was going on, he would have gone ballistic. So I was quietly and continually consumed with worry. To this day, I can not come to terms with, or forgive the fact that Ma put her needs before mine. And in doing so placed me, her son, in harm's way.

Chapter 9

First Love

Things began to change when I was seventeen going on eighteen. We were all still living at home, and unlike when I was younger, I wasn't afraid of Ken or Joan. I was well able to stand up for myself if confronted. Rita came into her own as a very outgoing and gregarious young lady, and everyone loved her, including me. Some evenings when we came home from work, she'd drag me up to dance in the kitchen to the sounds of Brendan Bowyer's Hucklebuck. She and Joan used to go dancing in the Ierne Ballroom just off Parnell Square where they'd have a good chance of meeting a "nice country boy," per Ma's guidance. At home they were always fighting over clothes, Rita used to borrow Joan's without asking, much to Joan's annoyance.

Meanwhile, Ken was an apprentice turner and fitter, a job he hated. Drawing was what he liked to do, and he was very good at it. He compiled a portfolio securing him a position as a graphic artist in RTE, the National Television Station, which was a great achievement. To me, though, he became even more insufferable once he got this job. When I was in the Corner House and saw him pass by on his way to RTE, I used to wave at him, but he purposely ignored me. What a snob, I thought. I was always hoping to connect with my older brother, but he never gave me an opening. He always treated me as if I was shit on his shoe. Coinciding with Ken's new job, a fancy red motorbike with drop handlebars appeared parked in our good room. This was the room that was off-limits to the rest of us even to sit in. How ridiculous! It was parked there each night for safety, and we were warned against touching it by Ma and Ken. This reconfirmed his special status in the family and added fuel to the resentment fire.

My twin sister Philomena and I had very little in common. Our attitudes to life and people were poles apart. She was very needy and asked too much of me, never feeling any inclination to return a favour. She tried to mimic Joan's authoritative attitude but lacked the commitment and fell short every time. Michael was the quiet one in the family and kept to himself inside and outside the house. He had learned very early on to keep a low profile to avoid trouble. I used to take him and Philomena to the pictures with me occasionally, and I always felt a sense of responsibility for Michael. However, as a young man, he sought to emulate Ken, the "arty-farty" one.

Eventually, Ken, Joan, and Michael adopted Ma's grandiose demeanour. They even cultivated a posh accent. Rita and myself, in comparison, were considered to be "common" and "over-familiar" with our neighbours. They made us feel that we were letting the family down. However, the six of us managed to survive in this small house, living parallel lives and seldom interacting. Rita was the first to leave home, going for what we thought was a week's holiday in England with her boyfriend. She didn't come back until three years later when she was married and had a new baby boy. Ma and Da didn't bother to go to her wedding, but Joan and Ken made the trip. They were joined by some of our cousins who were living in England at the time.

I was almost eighteen before I began to hang around with people my own age in the local area. Among these was Martin Carr, who I had met playing soccer in Herbert Park. Others in our larger circle of friends were the Egans, the Buckleys, Shay Geoghegan, Brendan Ash, Donal Conroy, and Brian O'Connor. As most of them were full-time students, we used to get together in the evenings and chat or sometimes go to the pictures on Sunday afternoons. I couldn't bring friends home to my house, because Ma had made it clear they wouldn't be welcome. On the odd occasion they did call for me, she would tell them to wait outside, close the door in their faces and then come to get me. "Your friends are at the door," she would say, condescendingly. I would race to the door and go straight out, furious with her for treating them so disrespectfully, but I had learned not to argue with her. I did spend time in their houses, however, and very soon it began to register with me how different our family lives were. I envied the relationships they had with their parents and the freedom they had to come and go as they pleased.

On the home front, I was gaining confidence to express my own opinions. Despite the newfound sense of independence, I still didn't have a key to the house and had to make excuses when out with my friends to leave early. The deadline to be home was nine o clock, or the door would have been bolted, and I was conditioned to know this wasn't an idle threat. I used to tell my friends that I had to take care of my younger brother, as I was embarrassed and ashamed to tell them the truth. I would have been a laughing stock, and my credibility in Donnybrook shot. Nevertheless, we met up fairly regularly and would congregate around a café in Rathmines, which was the "in place" for teenagers to hang out. The only problem was you needed money to sit down and order a coffee or soft drink, and we were rarely in a position to do that. Whenever we had money, it was the first place we headed; we loved it.

As time went by, it became clear to me that I had a better connection with Brian O'Connor than with my other friends. Brian was five foot two inches with a great mop of blond hair and

I was over six foot by then and had become quite skinny. We were like Mutt and Jeff. He looked like one of the guys from the Rolling Stones, which happened to be his favourite groups. We were different in so many ways but just got each other, and cherished this newfound friendship. We dreamed the same dreams and spent many hours walking the streets together and planning our futures. We talked about setting up a property company together—he would take care of the building, I would do the selling, and we'd share everything fifty-fifty. Then, of course, we both wanted to find and marry wonderful girls and agreed we would go on holidays together to our neighbouring vacation homes. We could go on for hours with these dreams, walking around the streets of Donnybrook with barely a few pennies in our pockets.

It was around this same time, at the Corner House, that I first became interested in the opposite sex. One moment I was purely focused on work, movies, and my friends, and the next I was captivated by Ann, the daughter of a customer from Nutley Road. She came in regularly with her parents to shop, and I'd use the excuse of fixing tins on the shelves, to follow her around the store. This did not go unnoticed. One day, I saw Tom Spain, the shop manager, smiling and wagging his finger at me as if to say, "I know what's going on." I was mortified and raced out to the storeroom, sheepishly returning when I had regained my composure. Determined to talk with Ann, I eventually overcame the butterflies in my stomach and went for it. I asked her name and what school she went to, desperately trying to get her to engage with me. The smile she gave me lit up her whole face and told me my approach was not unwelcome. Suddenly, I was walking on air and couldn't wait to see her again. Whenever she came in, we chatted, all small-talk. After a few weeks, when I discovered that she regularly went to Blackrock baths, I suggested we go there for a swim together.

We met in Blackrock, crossed over the railway bridge and headed toward the Baths. Once through the entrance style, Ann went into the girls dressing room, and I went into the boys. When I next saw her, she was walking toward the six-feet pool. I looked on longingly, wanting to join her, but it was the shallow children's pool for me. That's right, I didn't know how to swim. Nevertheless, this didn't deter me from going every week to spend some precious time with her. After the swim, we used to sit up on the benches overlooking the pool and chat about everything. One day when she didn't turn up, I took the opportunity to brave the deep pool and try and cross from one side to the other. I was terrified but determined to teach myself how to swim. After many attempts and the consumption of gallons of pool water, I finally made it, a complete width of the pool. I could not wait for the next time when Ann would be there.

As anticipated, she was amazed when she walked toward the adult pool, and I followed her and stepped down into the water. She asked me what I was doing, and I announced with confidence that I was going for a swim. As it turns out, it takes a bit longer than one day of practice to become a competent swimmer. But I splashed and spluttered as fast as I could to get to the other side, my pride winning out over any fear of drowning.

One day Ann told me that her family was going to Wicklow for their summer holidays. Without considering what a challenge this would be for me, I said I would visit her there. We arranged to meet at the Monument in the town on Sunday afternoon at two o'clock. That day, when the bus driver told me it would take two hours to get there, fear suddenly gripped me. I wasn't accustomed to travelling outside Dublin on my own. All I could think was, I'm going to get lost. I couldn't afford to miss the bus back and not be at work the next day. Overwhelmed by my anxieties, I lost my nerve and reluctantly got off the bus. I then went to see a movie in town to get my mind off of this terrible defeat. Suffice to say, I never made it to the Monument, and stood Ann up in the process. I had let her and myself down. Our relationship ended abruptly before it even got a chance to take off. It would be years before we met again. I do not know how things would have worked out if I had gone that day, but I have nothing but lovely memories of our times together. Ann was my first love, but we never actually kissed, I couldn't muster the courage. I was too shy and insecure to make a move despite my best efforts.

My social life really kicked off when I started to go dancing with my mates in the Hall at the Mary Magdalene Convent. This was run by the nuns who also operated the Magdalene Laundry. This was staffed by what was known as "fallen women" who were placed to their care. The church encouraged the locals to support the nuns and bring their washing there. Ma used to send us up with large items, such as sheets and blankets, warning us not to talk with any of these "bad" women ". There was an air of mystery about their confinement. But nobody ever saw them in the village or asked any questions, trusting that the nuns were doing the right thing. It would be years before the abuse they were subjected to, became public knowledge.

The dances organised by the nuns for local teenagers were on Friday evenings. Parents felt secure that we were safe in their hands, so they never objected to us going. The Dance would start at 7pm sharp with prayers, and throughout the evening, the nuns would walk around the dance floor to make sure there was "fresh air" separating the dancing couples. No "lurching" was allowed. This, needless to say, did not stop us, so the nuns were kept busy. The Dance would end on the dot of 9 pm with the National Anthem. While this was playing, if anyone was disrespectful, they would be barred from the dances. Despite the strict "rules", these were great nights. The music was new and exciting to me, and I was mixing with fellow teenagers, especially girls. We considered this dance hall ours, our place to socialise. Friday nights could not come soon enough!

If at one of these dances, you happened to hook up with a girl and started doing a line, that was a bonus. To secure the status of going steady with somebody, you had to kiss her. For teenagers new to the game, this demanded a lot of courage and perseverance. But the great sense of achievement and the reward of going back to your mates to report success was well worth the effort. Because, if you said you had never done a line before, that meant you'd never kissed a girl. Lines often only lasted a few weeks before you or the girl would move on to another prospect.

At one time, I was lucky enough to have two girls interested in me. Very juvenile stuff. As would be, my mind couldn't cope with this marvellous dilemma. So to help me decide which one to go steady with they suggested I go to a film they had heard about where a guy was in love with two girls. The fact that ours was a simple crush on each other was beside the point. So off I went on my own to see Dr Zhivago. This turned out to be the best film I had ever seen, thoroughly enjoyable with fantastic scenery, music, and what a storyline. Before I knew it, the film was over, and I hadn't given a thought to the girls. I had planned to meet one of them in Donnybrook on my way home, and when I got there, I was surprised to find them both waiting for me, and all they wanted to know was had I made my mind up. I told them I was still confused (having found the film far more interesting than the impending decision). "Well, let us help you out with that one, then " they replied, and both girls dropped me instantly. I was left there standing on my own a little deflated, but somewhat relieved that the decision was made.

I had no difficulty getting over this episode, as I had my eye on another girl called Eithne. After a few weeks, we were going steady, and I was flying high again. We often used to go to the pictures in town, in the afternoons and once, before the film, I took her to Cafola's Café on O'Connell Street. To impress, I ordered a Knickerbocker glory for her. When it was put in front of us, she blushed at the sight of this exotic dessert. It was served in a very tall glass with a long-handled spoon and filled with layers of ice cream, fruit, whipped cream, syrups and two fan-like wafers perched on top. I enjoyed watching her tackle this enormous feast as she approached it, cautiously at first but then succumbing to the mouth sensation. My job was done, she was suitably impressed.

Eithne was the first girl I kissed. I was eighteen. It took me a few weeks to get around to it, but finally, I got my chance. We were out for a walk, and I brought her to a well-known spot where young couples could get some privacy. This was a lane that ran behind the houses on Morehampton Road. It took me some time to muster the courage, but eventually, after much fumbling, l managed a feeble kiss. Not content with the first attempt I went in again and this time . . . mission accomplished. I was quite proud of myself only to discover later that Eithne considered she had committed a sin and that evening had gone straight to church to confess. We had some good fun together, but after about six weeks, I was gazumped by Martin Carr who, unknown to me, had been making moves on her behind my back. I was shattered by the betrayal and disloyalty, and it took me some time to come to terms and get over it. This was a blow to my confidence and also to my trust in my newfound friends.

With my confidence damaged, I was feeling down. I didn't want to have to explain to the guys what happened with Eithne. So rather than go out and meet up with them, I was hanging around the house. Ma and Da were in the kitchen and seemed to be getting on very well chatting together. Out of the blue, I heard her say to him, "Patrick needs a suit, you should take him into town and buy him one." I didn't know what prompted her to ask this. Maybe it was because she knew he was cash-rich after a lucky streak. I didn't expect him to agree and was shocked when he did. We walked up to the village, side by side, me and my Dad, which was a first for us. By now, I was almost as tall as my father but, unlike him, was very skinny. He looked smart as usual in his overcoat and hat. I wore a jumper and light-green Levi's jeans, my casual wear, the best clothes I owned. As we stood at the bus stop to get the number 10 bus to O'Connell Street, my excitement and sense of pride were building.

When the bus arrived I hopped on and eagerly looked out the window as we made our way to town. Once we reached our stop, my father led me to a tailor shop called Weaver to Wearer on Henry Street, where he told the assistant that he was here to buy a suit for his son. Music to my ears. I checked out the offerings and settled on a three-piece navy suit and, to match, a woven tie, which was the height of fashion. As far as I was concerned, I was becoming James Bond. The shop assistant wrapped the purchases in brown paper and, as I walked out of the shop, with my parcel under my arm, I felt like a million bucks.

The last time I had a new suit was for my Confirmation when I was thirteen, and it had been a source of great embarrassment. Ma had bought it for me six months early to spread the costs as she also had to buy an outfit for Philomena. However, by the time the Confirmation Day came along, I had put on weight, and the trousers didn't fit. Ma had to cut the seam at the back of the waistband and insert a v-shaped piece of material. Unfortunately, it did not match, so I was warned not to put my hands in my pockets in case I exposed the clearly identifiable patch. As if that was not enough, the trousers were short while everyone else had long ones. I stood out like a sore thumb and felt totally humiliated. This time was different, though. I had picked my own suit, it was super trendy, and I had just had my first one-on-one outing with my father. I couldn't have felt happier, and I made a point to express this joy as soon as we stepped out onto the street and thanked Da for his gift. He looked at me, and with that wry smile of his, said, "Well, as soon as you can save up the money, you can pay me back." His reply took me by complete surprise. I went from being ecstatic to absolutely gutted. What I wanted to do right there and then was throw the suit in the gutter and tell him to "fuck off". But I swallowed my pride and buried my pain, not wanting to give Da the satisfaction of seeing how he had hurt me.

The journey home was silent and felt endless. Da had taken what I had believed was our special day and turned it into shit, and there was nothing I could do. It wasn't just a suit, to me, I had mistakingly thought it was a sign of affection and maybe even of love. But he had bought it under pressure from Ma, and resented her and me for this, making sure I was fully aware that this was not of his choosing. On that day, I promised myself that

Confirmation Day 1962

My Neighbour's son, Chris and me.

Philomena & Me

if I ever had a son, he would never feel pain like this. On the positive side, I got many years of pleasure strutting around Donnybrook in my 007 suit.

An unexpected thing happened soon after, this time attacking my fragile ego. One morning, as I was looking in the mirror while shaving, I noticed my hair seemed to be receding, and I froze. Alarm bells started going off in my head. *I am going bald!* I thought. It didn't help that for years beforehand my Da had been telling me that if I didn't stop scratching my head, I wouldn't have a screed of hair by the time I was twenty-one. As my father was bald himself, I believed him to be an expert on the subject. So my worst fears seemed to be turning into reality. *I am going to be bald,* I thought. *None of my heroes are bald . . . how will I ever get a girl to marry me? What a feckin' disaster!*

Each morning as I shaved, I was constantly reminded that I was just one day closer to baldness. Shaving became tortuous and looking in mirrors was to be avoided. I became so self-conscious that anytime a girl put a hand near my head, I pulled it away immediately: she couldn't know my secret. When I got a bit older and had some money, I went to a hair clinic for baldness, in Grafton St. Here my head was massaged with potions, by a gorgeous girl in a white coat. This was very enjoyable. But after a few weeks, I couldn't see any benefit and felt it was an expensive con, so I never went back.

I then began to self-prescribe and tried out loads of creams and lotions from the pharmacy, purporting to restore hair loss. Nothing worked, my hair was still well back on my head, so I gave in. The only thing left to me was prayer, and I also tried this, every night, and it definitely gave me comfort. As it turned out, impending baldness was not my problem, it was a high forehead, which I inherited from Ma's side of the family. Thanks Granda!

Chapter 10

Finding Courage

It was time for a change. I had been working at the Corner House for two years, doing a man's job, and was experienced in every department. I then discovered that the rest of the staff were earning more than double my salary for doing similar work. I was on six pounds a week, five pounds and ten shillings of this going to Ma, not leaving much for me. So armed with encouragement from my co-workers, and the need to right the wrong, I decided to approach Mr Wilka for a wage increase. Mr Wilka listened while I made my case. "Let me see what I can do," he said. "I will let you know by the end of the week." I left his office filled with pride, knowing I had done the right thing, and confident my efforts and my hard work would be rewarded.

When Friday arrived, I eagerly opened my wage packet, filled with excitement and sky-high expectations. But when I looked inside, my heart sank. Six pounds, ten shillings. Only ten shillings raise. What? My co-workers were earning double that, and I was just as good if not better at the job. My disappointment soon turned to anger, and before I knew it, I was standing in Mr Wilka's office. "I think there is a mistake in my wages," I said with sheer frustration. "No," he said, "that's your pay increase." Noticing my dissatisfaction, he added, "In my opinion, that is a good increase. You should be happy." Happy? Happy about a ten shillings increase? No way. It was now clear to me that I wasn't as highly valued as my other co-workers. I wasn't happy. I was frustrated and downright angry. Yet, as I walked out of his office, I buried my emotions and put on my best face, knowing at that moment that it was time to look for a new job.

Meanwhile, life at home was bearable, but for the fact that Ma was still using me as a pawn in her rows with Da. Once, I overheard them fighting, and she said in complete frustration, "Your gambling is more important to you than your family. If I didn't get money from Patrick, we'd go hungry!" It was a strange thing to hear her say. I felt a pang of pride, inadvertently receiving a compliment from Ma. She didn't mean to praise me but to humiliate him. He was a proud man, and those comments must have hurt him. Sadly, no matter what herculean efforts I made over the years to build a good father-son relationship, Ma poisoned any chance there was of this. She consistently used me to get at him, and I was just collateral damage in their animosity towards each other.

Then it happened, the thing I had most feared since I was a child—and right when I was beginning to feel more relaxed with an inkling of independence at home, right when I had let my guard down. I had just come back from the Corner House after a long day's work and was sitting at the dinner table arguing with Philomena about God knows what. I had a knife and fork in my hands and was about to dig into my food. Next minute my father abruptly said, "Who are you pointing that knife at?" Before I could even answer, he was by my side, yanking me out of the chair and pushing me up against the wall. In the blink of an eye, I suddenly felt his hands around my throat choking me. As I struggled for air, all I could see was hate and viciousness in his eyes. Terror permeated my heart followed quickly by a burst of courage, which demanded I stop him. I put my two hands around my father's wrists and, with all the strength I could muster, began to pull his arms apart and away from my throat, all the while staring him down. Fury turned to fear in Da's blue eyes. Neither of us knew up until that moment how strong I had become from years of lifting heavy sacks of potatoes on the horse and cart.

When his hands were at a safe distance from my throat, I released my iron grip from his wrists. Without a word, he turned and walked out of the kitchen in shock.

I think he feared what I might do to him, but he didn't know me at all. If he had, he would have known I would not lift a finger to hurt him. My problem with my father was that no matter how hard I tried to show him I loved him, he blocked all my attempts as if he was swatting a fly. He was not prepared to invest any time or emotion in me, and now the thought that he had tried to kill me was absolutely unbearable. I had been living in fear of the day when he would turn on me as he had done with Ma all those years ago. But when the time finally came, I was strong enough to defend myself. He had waited too long. I had survived, but a piece of me died that day.

For some reason, Ma wasn't at home that day. So in desperation, I ran up to the village and phoned my older sister Joan. Unable to hold back the tears, I pleaded with her to let me come and stay with her for the night, but she told me there was no room there for me. I felt let down but should have known better. I just had nowhere else to go. I walked the streets for hours until I came to terms with the fact that I had no choice but to face whatever consequences awaited me at home. By the time I got back, I had readied myself to defend my position, but not a word was said by anyone—it was as if nothing had happened.

I went to bed that night, terrified. Lying awake, I waited for Da to get up and lunge across the room in a full-blown attack, but this time I wouldn't be caught off-guard. Next thing I knew it was morning and nothing had happened. Elated and relieved, I got up and went to work as usual. It was over, and I had summoned the courage to stand up for myself, with impressive strength. I was so proud of myself and would never allow anyone to beat me again. I felt like Gary Cooper in *High Noon,* I was walking tall.

Shortly after, I heard that an up and coming supermarket group called Five Star, based in Tullamore, had opened branches in Dublin and was looking for trainee managers. Open interviews were being held at their new store in Rathmines, and I went for it. Fortunately, no paperwork was required to be completed in advance, which was a great relief to me as reading and writing continued to be my secret Achilles' heel.

The following Thursday at eleven in the morning, I sat in a waiting room, ready to be interviewed. I had never been to such an office before. Anger had been my driving force. I was angry with Mr Wilka for not valuing my work, with my colleagues who had encouraged me to speak up, and with myself for failing. But then it hit me. What the hell am I doing here? Panic-stricken, I suddenly realised that I had never actually done a formal job interview before. I didn't even know how to prepare for one . . .

and what if they actually gave me the job? That would involve change. The life I had worked so hard to have, with my great colleagues and customers, was suddenly up in the air. And all because of me. Was I really prepared to give it all up and jump into the unknown?

Before I knew it, an office door opened and a lean, well-dressed man, invited me to come in. He introduced himself as Mr O'Connor, the area manager. When he began to ask me questions about myself, I began to feel a little more at ease. As the interview progressed, the questions became more specific, focusing on the operation of a grocery store. Although I had all the relevant experience, anxiety took over, my mind went blank, and I froze. When Mr O'Connor started to talk, I was hanging on his every word. "Unfortunately, to join our trainee manager program, you would need to have a Leaving Certificate." he said, "But I can offer you a job on our delicatessen counter. The basic salary is eighteen pounds a week, and you can earn overtime for working late nights." That was more than three times what I was getting at the Corner House! I couldn't say yes, fast enough. We shook hands, and I left the office all smiles and with an extra bounce in my step. Filled with pride and a renewed sense of worth, I gave Mr Wilka a week's notice. I left the Corner House having exchanged the bare minimum of words with him—he had lost interest in me, and the feeling was mutual.

Within the first couple of weeks working at Five Star, it was clear that I knew a lot more about the business than I had been able to get across during the interview. But I had nothing to worry about—now my work was speaking for itself. My new manager was very pleased with my broad knowledge, my experience, and most importantly, my insatiable appetite for work. I approached every task with energy and enthusiasm and was moved from department to department, whenever extra help was needed. I got to know the staff quickly and really enjoyed being part of this big team. Everyone supported each other and jobs, working hours, and conditions were all clearly defined. At the Corner House, there was a small team, working directly with very demanding owners. This created a tense atmosphere when they were around, which was most of the time. On the other hand, their uncompromising approach to discipline and delivering the highest service made sure that we were working at the top of our game at all times. This work ethic became ingrained in me, and I will always be thankful for the training and grounding I got at the Corner House.

Two months after starting my new job, Mr O'Connor called into the supermarket. When he saw me, he shook my hand, congratulating me saying that he had heard nothing but positive reports about me. I was floating on cloud nine. Within a short time, my life had changed dramatically for the best. It was my first lesson on how to embrace change rather than fear it. I was working at an organisation that appreciated me and paid me accordingly. And also earning enough to buy Ma whatever she asked for, without putting myself in harm's way, no thanks to her. The relief that came from this was priceless. Ma was also happier because I continued to hand over the majority of my wages. This meant she was better off, and I was slowly inching toward my freedom.

I was so excited about my new job and the opportunities lining up before me that I decided to attend evening classes at the School of Retail Distribution in Parnell Square. I wanted to learn as much as I could about the business I knew and loved. One thing I didn't anticipate was the networking opportunity these classes offered. I made numerous valuable contacts, many of whom I would later encounter again as my career developed. To top it off, I received my very own Certificate in Commerce.

Because I was now working late nights as well as attending evening classes, my deadline to be home was lifted. I still didn't get my own key to the house and used the one left on a string inside the letterbox. There was no direct bus route to Rathmines, and it would have been great to have a bike for travelling to and from work. But not surprisingly, Ma refused to let me have one, so I walked the two miles. It did occur to me that maybe, like Ken, I should get a flat of my own. I was earning enough to afford it and all my colleagues, who were from the country, were in digs. So why not? Each time I came close to making a move, I could hear Ma's words ringing in my ears *"Who will look after you, what if you lose your job, how will you survive? If you leave this house there will be no coming back, there will be no bed for you here."* The memory of being locked out as a child was never far from my mind. I didn't dare to break away.

Chapter 11

Great Love and a Giant Loss

Late June 1968 found me working at the Five Star Supermarket on Baggot Street, in the Bacon and Delicatessen department. Beside my counter was the butcher's which was managed by Pat Tansey. To lighten up the atmosphere and have some fun, we used to alert each other if we saw a beautiful girl come into the store. One day, my heart skipped a beat, when I saw, what looked like a film star walking toward me. The shelves and stock disappeared, and all I could see was this vision. As luck would have it, she was shopping for sliced cooked ham, and my counter was her destinations. I made it my business to serve her, engaging all my charms, giving her my best smile, and pulling out all the stops to catch her attention. She seemed shy and reserved, which made me even more attracted to her, but none of what I did seemed to be registering. Nothing. All she did was politely take her purchase and leave my counter. I watched her walk away, stunned by her Sophia Loren–like beauty, thinking, *Well, she looks just as good walking away as she did walking in.*

The next day she came in again. I enthusiastically alerted Pat, "Look, she's back! Jesus, I'd love to ask her out." He immediately responded, "I bet you a pound you don't." This was all the encouragement I needed. When she approached the counter, it was to complain about the meat I had given her the day before. I was genuinely mortified and apologised profusely. I offered her a refund or a replacement, and she opted for the replacement. I headed to the slicing machine and then came back to the counter, and took my time wrapping the package up so I could look at her and be in her company. "Not only will I replace it," I said, and mustering all my courage I added, "but I'd love to take you out. Would you like to come?" To my surprise and delight, she said yes!

There was a local dance on Wednesday evenings in Belvedere Rugby Club, a popular venue for teenagers in those days, so I invited her to come with me. She had told me her name was Pauline, but I incorrectly called her Paula, and she was too polite to correct me. We arranged to meet at the phone box outside Donnybrook Church and, true to form, I was there early waiting for her when she arrived. She had golden skin, warm brown eyes and a shy stride that revealed she was absolutely unaware of her stunning beauty. We had plenty of time to get to the dance, so we went for a walk around Donnybrook. Within a few minutes, she told me that she shouldn't have agreed to meet as she had a boyfriend who was away in the United States for the summer, earning money for college. No matter how many times I tried to change the subject, I could see she was apprehensive about being out with me and it looked as if she was going to call a halt to the night. I was furiously thinking, how I could deal with this and put her at her ease. Then a thought struck me, so I took a chance and said, "I understand about your boyfriend, but I am not looking for a steady girlfriend. Come September I'll be busy with night classes and late nights at work." Then I added, "We can just be friends and hang out together until your boyfriend gets back." My powers of persuasion worked beautifully, and she agreed on these terms. I had no intention of doing any night classes, but I knew I had to come up with something. I didn't want to let this girl go. After a good night at the dance, we arranged to go to the cinema the following weekend.

During the following weeks, we met about twice a week, and later more often. She lived in Booterstown, a bus ride from Donnybrook, and I used to go out to her house to collect her for our dates. One day Pauline was telling me how much she loved the Beatles and asked which of their records I liked best. I didn't know any of them, so rather than embarrass myself, I answered that I preferred Elvis. In fact, in our house, we were not allowed to choose what to listen to on the radio. The only music we heard at home was whatever our Ma or Da wanted. There was no question of any of us playing a transistor radio or record player, of our own, in the house even though we could have afforded it. So my music influence was mainly Dermot O'Brien and the Howdowners, Bridie Gallagher, and Jim Reeves. But Elvis was everywhere, and Rita loved him, so he inevitably seeped into my ears.

On my way home that evening, I decided to find out more about the Beatles. Although what should have been, my carefree teenage years were nearly over, I still had a lot of learning to do, especially when it came to popular music. Now I was going to start living for today rather than dreaming about the future. We went to dances, the cinema, bowling, and Bray seaside attractions. Our Sunday afternoon outings to the cinema on Grafton Street were magical. They were showing a string of old movies, so we had the chance to see classics such as The Great Waltz, a 1938 film based on the life of Johann Strauss. The music was intoxicating. Other favourites were Nelson Eddie and Jeanette Mc Donald, and Ginger Rogers and Fred Astaire movies. They were spectacular —all filled with romance, which eventually influenced the course of our relationship.

A few weeks into our friendship, while climbing up to Bray Head, I got my first chance to make a pass at her. She was wearing a round-necked T-shirt, and as I reached down to help her along, I couldn't help but see her soft firm cleavage. She, in her innocence, was oblivious to this, which made it even more appealing. Encouraged by a wave of undeniable desire, when we lay down to rest in the sun, I went in for a kiss. I was very awkward and clumsy, but at last, I got there, and it was well worth the effort. Her lips were soft and tender, and we had crossed a line —now I considered her my girlfriend. The rest of the summer was idyllic, full of joy, laughter and fun as we learned more about each other.

One day we were walking up to the Bowling Alley in nearby Stillorgan, and she mentioned she'd be having a birthday party in a few weeks and would I come. "Of course, I'd love to go," I said, overjoyed, never having been to a birthday party. "What age will you be?" I added, thinking she'd say seventeen or eighteen. "Sixteen," she replied. I was absolutely dumbfounded. *What! She's only fifteen!* I thought. *She's only a child! Four years younger than me! What will Pat Tansey think? What will the guys think? I'll be accused of cradle snatching?*

My mind was in turmoil. I knew she would be going back to school in September, but it never occurred to me that she was that young. My immediate reaction was to get her home and end the relationship. Not wanting her to see my shock, I suggested we walk back and give the bowling alley a miss. I didn't want to be seen out with a fifteen-year-old, though obviously I didn't say this to her. Thankfully, by the time we reached her house, I had calmed down. I decided she was too important to me to let her age break us up. I couldn't be without her. She had no idea how far I had come on that walk home. But to preserve my credibility, I decided I wouldn't volunteer her age to anyone and, if asked, I would say she was seventeen.

Then one night while walking home from the pictures she turned to me and said, "By the way, Billy's home tomorrow and I want to go back to him." I almost replied "Billy who?" until it hit me: Billy, the boyfriend! I had come to believe that he was long gone and had not even given him a second thought until that night. Panic struck, and my heart sank. I hadn't considered this possibility—she had caught me completely off guard and words failed me. I quickly ordered my thoughts. I knew her well enough by then to understand she hadn't made such a decision lightly, so begging her to stay would be pointless. We continued to walk in silence until we reached her house where I reluctantly put my hand out to shake hers, and said, "I've had a great summer. Thanks very much." I could not think of anything else to add, so I turned and walked away without a fight, shaken to my core. As I left her side to get the bus home, my legs were buckling beneath me, but I somehow managed to muster the strength to move forward. I was in absolute shock, my heart breaking with every step. When I reached the end of her avenue, for a split second, I thought to myself, *What are you doing? Go back. I don't care, beg her to stay.* But I resisted the urge and continued on my way home.

After what felt like a never-ending, sleepless night, I headed into work exhausted, totally confused, and feeling like a total a wreck. All I wanted to do was phone her and beg her to come back. I didn't care how pathetic this was, I had to do it. The store manager would not let me make a personal call from his office, so I would have to wait until after work to call her. I spent the whole day in frustration and foul humour; minutes felt like hours. I wanted to talk to Pat Tansey about it but was afraid I might break down and couldn't stand that humiliation on top of the turmoil already in my heart. I thought about what I would say when I called her and changed it a thousand times over. My instinct told me this was a huge mistake, but my heart overruled my head.

On the dot at six o'clock, I rushed out the door and made for the public phone box across the road when I suddenly heard a voice calling, "Pat . . . Pat." I quickly turned around to see Pauline standing there before me. Her next words were music to my ears, the sweetest five words I would ever hear, "Will you take me back?" This from the loveliest black-haired, brown-eyed beauty with golden skin. I was in ecstasy. Now my mind and body were in turmoil again, but this was a positive turmoil. "Of course I will," I said in sheer happiness, a feeling and a moment that will live with me forever.

That night, we went to the local chipper to celebrate, and I walked on air all the way home. I had girlfriends before but never one like this. She was the most enchanting girl I had ever met and still is today. We started from very different places, but Pauline was very patient, caring, and loving in every way. She allowed me the time (a very long time) to grow and learn from my mistakes. She made me feel special, and the only thing she wanted was for me to be happy. For whatever reason, I had found someone who loved me for me, and nothing else.

All of this was happening when my home life was full of arguments and tension. None of my family was interested in hearing about my Pauline. But this relationship meant I only went home to sleep there and in time I wouldn't even be doing that. When I think of all the unbelievably sad and cruel days, I could never have dreamed this would happen to me. But here I was making it happen myself, for myself.

Around the same time that I met Pauline, my best friend, Brian, started to go out with a girl called Joyce. We both had girlfriends now and talked about getting married and visiting each other's families in the future. He was going to be a builder and I a top-class salesman, and we still had dreams of joining forces, forming a company, and running the business together. Even though we hadn't a clue how to go about it, we walked and talked about it for hours on end, determined to make it happen. Everything seemed possible. We were slowly on our way out of our homes and into the world. The excitement and anticipation of what the future had in store for us were coursing through our veins.

I was beginning to gain confidence in my abilities and entered a new phase in my relationship with Ma when we talked very little. She had no interest in my work life or my personal life. As long as I handed her the money every week, she seemed content. For her, the past was the past, to be forgotten and never to be talked about. For me, it was impossible to forget. I began to put distance between us, but still would have done anything for her. She was my Ma, and I loved her.

There was only one time I had a row with her, it was when I was about nineteen. I got home from work starving, as usual. Ma put my dinner on the table, and I began to devour it. As I sat there focused on my food, she started to complain about Pauline. "She is only interested in you because you have money, as soon as she leaves school she'll be gone." I tried to ignore her digs, but she persisted and wouldn't let it go. I kept eating and said nothing, but the anger was slowly rising until I finally erupted, banging my fists down on the formica table and sending my dinner plate flying through the air with a crash landing on the floor beside me. "You know nothing about Pauline," I said, furiously. "You won't even let her inside the front door! So you're not entitled to have an opinion. I never want to hear you talk about Pauline again." She was absolutely stunned, and before she could say anything else, I started to pick the broken pieces of plate and food off the floor. All I could think about was my dinner, *What am I going to do for food now?* Once I finished cleaning up, I raced up to the village chipper—chips never tasted so good. As I sat outside eating, it suddenly dawned on me: I was finally free of Ma. For years I had lived in fear, but that seminal day marked the beginning of the end. Ma had felt my strength and courage for the first time. I was a lion, I had found my voice and wasn't afraid to use it. Things at home would never be the same again.

Later that year, my world was turned upside down. I was at home one day when Martin Carr called to the door unexpectedly. Ma answered it and brought him into the front room, which was unusual, so I immediately suspected something was wrong. I rushed in to hear a stunned Martin say that Brian O'Connor was dead. My heart stopped, and I was frozen in shock. Apparently, Brian was going into town on the bus with his girlfriend, Joyce, to have his hair cut. They were sitting on the upper level of a double-decker bus when he collapsed, without any warning. She tried to resuscitate him but to no avail and there was nothing anyone could do. We later found out that his heart had been weakened when he had contracted rheumatic fever as a schoolboy.

His sudden death, at such an early age, was absolutely inconceivable. I rushed out the door with Martin, and we ran up the road to where Brian lived. When the door opened, Brian's sister stood in front of me, looking ghostly, with tears rolling down her face. It was only then that I knew for sure Brian was gone. I must have been in a terrible state because she brought me into the front room and sat me down. I remember crying uncontrollably into my hands, with my head bent down to my knees, as it registered that I would never see or speak with him again. The room was packed with family and friends, including some of Brian's other close friends, who had flocked to offer condolences and support. There was no sign of his parents, they were too distraught and broken hearted to meet anyone. It was left to his two sisters to receive the mourners. How they coped I will never know, they were magnificent.

When I managed to compose myself, my immediate instinct was to go to Pauline, I had to tell her, I needed her now. But I had no way to get there, and I had no money. Shay

Geoghegan saw my distress and understood my desperation. He offered me his Honda, and even though I had never been on a motorbike before, I took him up on the offer. He showed me how to put it in first gear and work the throttle and off I went. I took it easy at first and felt quite confident as I drove through Donnybrook out toward the Stillorgan Road. Going past the Corner House, even in my state of grief, I couldn't help but glance through the window to see if anyone was watching. I could hardly believe it myself. Here was I on a motorbike, a Honda! I was exhilarated and terrified, but I wanted my ex-colleagues to see this "rebel" as I glided past.

As my confidence grew so did the pain in my heart, so I picked up speed to get to Pauline as soon as possible. I had no helmet, and the noise of the engine rang in my ears. Suddenly, the bike weaved from side to side, and I was very close to crashing into a van. A wake-up call if there ever was one, I was abruptly aware that I could have easily been killed. The remainder of the journey was terrifying, so I slowed to a crawl and travelled extra close to the footpath, at times using my foot on the curb to keep me steady.

When I finally got to Pauline, she put her arms around me, and we cried together. This was, without a doubt, the worst day of my life so far. Nothing made sense to me. Brian was my best friend, and I had genuinely loved him as such. When I returned home that evening, I was clearly perturbed, desperately needing my mother's love and understanding. When she heard that I had gone directly from Brian's house to see Pauline, she was annoyed and immediately closed up. The fact that I had just lost my best friend meant nothing to her. I tried to express the depth of my loss, but she just looked at me with her all-too-familiar vacant face. In frustration, I started to cry, "How does an eighteen-year-old boy die like that? How can I stop this pain? I can't bear it." "If you are going to carry on like this, you should go to bed," she replied, coldly. I felt so fragile and was yearning so much for an ounce of her compassion, that her frigid demeanour burned deep into my, already broken, heart. From then on, I stopped telling her what was going on in my life. I didn't need or want her opinion on anything. Suddenly I felt released from the constant pressure to make her happy. We never talked about Brian again. Like so many things that were important to me, I had learned to keep them to myself, rather than allow her to sully them.

For quite a few months after Brian died, I visited his parents, believing this would bring some comfort to them and me. I felt I might be closer to him in their company, in his home. But it was soon clear to me that this wasn't helping. I was just another reminder to them of their loss, and their distress added to my pain, so I stopped calling. Likewise, with Joyce, I tried to involve her in my life with Pauline. But her depression and despair were such that she was never in the mood for company and we drifted apart. It took me many years to get over the pain of losing my one and only true male best friend. Fourteen years later, when our first son was born, Pauline and I named him Brian.

When I think of my friend now, I smile. I still miss him terribly and will never forget him. There were two promises I made to myself after that terrible period. The first was to live every day as if it was my last. The second, to never ride a motorbike again. To this date, I haven't broken either promise.

Chapter 12

Independence

My boss at Five Star was happy with my work and asked if I would help set up delicatessen departments and train staff in other branches. I was given a salary increase, and much more, a boost to my self-esteem. It wasn't long before Bon Vivant, one of our delicatessen suppliers, asked if I would like to become a sales representative with them. This was an opportunity to develop my natural sales skills at a totally different level, and I couldn't let it pass. But, I had a significant hurdle to overcome: I didn't know how to drive, and I didn't have a car. My hunger to succeed was such that I was prepared to do whatever it would take to get my licence as soon as possible. When I explained my predicament, the company said they would wait for me. The pressure was on, and it was time for action.

I set myself up with driving lessons but, after six of these, it was clear that without a car to practice in, they wouldn't be of much use. So for the first time ever, I turned to Da for help unaware that he was on the verge of selling his car in favour of free public transport. Because of his age, he was now entitled to a bus and rail pass. So my timing was perfect, and to my amazement, he agreed to take me out in his car that very day.

Our drive was intense from the second we left the curb, Da was obviously regretting his decision to take me out. Every time I changed gear, I could hear him mutter to himself in frustration. When he was not telling me to keep up with the traffic, it was slow down, you're going too fast. As we were approaching the gates of Phoenix Park, Da suddenly shouted in a total panic, "For fuck sake slow down, you'll take the fucking gates off the Pillars! Jesus Christ slow down!" This completely distracted me, and I must have put my foot on the accelerator because we went through the gates like Sterling Moss. Shock doesn't adequately describe the state we were both in, but at least the Pillars were still intact. From that moment on Da cursed and complained all the way, "What are you trying to do, put the fucking gear stick through the fucking windscreen?" he screamed, as I struggled to change gear to the sound of a screeching gearbox. He pleaded with me to surrender the car to him. But I knew this was my one and only shot to get the experience I needed to get the final rewards: a driver's license and a rep's job. So I kept going, determined to make the most of this opportunity. Da then suggested we proceed to some minor roads. Before we knew it, we were lost in the Dublin Mountains, navigating dirt tracks only suitable for one car at a time, fenced in by a bog on either side. In fear of meeting an oncoming car, I sped up, and my Da went ballistic again. "Can you not read the feckin' signposts, you're going in the wrong direction?" he shouted. I hadn't the nerve to tell him I didn't even see the signposts I was going that fast. "Stop the feckin' car!" he demanded. "No, I'm not stopping! I need to do this! You promised!" I yelled back in anger. In my mind, I had only one goal and my desire to achieve this was more powerful than any fear I had of my father and his cursing. Da and I had never exchanged so many words as we did on that drive, and they were mostly his.

When we eventually found our way home, it was four hours later. We were both shattered, and the look of relief on my Da's face said it all. Despite the heart-stopping experience and vitriolic diatribe, I cracked it. I was confident I could drive and never looked back. As I got out of the car, I turned to my Da and with my biggest smile, jokingly said, "Jesus Da, that was great, we should do it all again tomorrow." Da's smile reflected mine as he replied, "not in a million years son!" For a single solitary moment, father and son were on the same page. I will never forget that experience with my Da and my journey to freedom.

My cherished Hillman Imp. 1968

I was now ready to purchase my first car. I had £60 in savings, and my brother-in-law, Tony, kindly went guarantor for me to borrow an additional £70. I had enough to buy a used Hillman Imp at the Windsor Motors Car Auction. It had a radio and six month's guarantee. I was elated. This car changed my life. No more being caught in the rain. Bus timetables were a thing of the past, and I had much more flexibility in when and where I went. For the first time, I had a space of my own. At night I would sit outside the house listening to the radio until it was time to go to bed. The only thing I didn't do was sleep in it, and that thought had crossed my mind a few times. I had no idea what joy, independence, and freedom a car could bring.

I practised my driving at every spare moment and, even though I was well prepared when it was time to take my driving test, I struggled with anxiety. Passing the test was so important to me that I made some silly mistakes on my first two attempts, like, going left when I was asked to go right. I put this down to the fact that I had been forced to write with my right hand. I now didn't know my left from my feckin' right! On my third test, the engine cut out and I had to get out of the car, open the bonnet, and fix it. In fact, this was my saving grace. Because I was now more worried about the car cutting out again than I was of the examiner sitting beside me, I didn't make any driving mistakes.

Fortunately, the Rules of the Road were tested orally, and I flew through this test and was rewarded with a full driver's license. I was now ready to take up the sales representative position with Bon Vivant. As this job came with a company car, I sold my beloved Hillman Imp and prepared myself for what was to become a whole new adventure.

Bon Vivant was an importer of specialist foods from across Europe and the Soviet Block: beetroot and gherkins from Poland, pickled onions from Holland, sauerkraut from Germany, oils and sauces from Italy, and mixed salads from Bulgaria. My role was to introduce this exotic range to Delicatessens, Fine Food shops, and Hotels throughout the Republic of Ireland. I travelled the highways and byways in my company car, an Opel Kadett Estate, and got to know every town and village in the country. An overnight trip was often required, but I usually drove all the way home. My deep-seated insecurity and anxiety were so debilitating that I gave up the opportunity to stay in a hotel, where I would have the luxury of an ensuite room to myself. My behaviour was not unlike the elephant, that has been trained not to step outside the Circus ring. Even when the chain is removed from his ankle, he stays within the boundary. Like him, I was conditioned not to stray from home, but after many anxious attempts, I did eventually break free and began the long journey to release myself from Ma's controlling grip.

The whole delicatessen business was relatively new, but there was a lot of money to be made with specialist products like ours by buying in bulk and selling on, in portion sizes. Most of my customers had never even heard of these products, so they were not easy to sell. Luckily rejection was something I had learned to cope with. In hindsight, the challenge I faced pushed me to really sharpen my sales skills and, with persistence, I always exceeded my targets. I was in my element and loved securing the deals. My efforts were very much appreciated by the Directors of Bon Vivant, who made me feel part of their team. My opinions and recommendations were always welcomed at our weekly planning meetings. This job gave me great experience in cold calling and confirmed to me that I was a natural-born salesman. It also gave me prestige and for the first time in my working life, my weekends off, which meant more time with Pauline.

One of our favourite things to do on weekends was to head off around Ireland in her car. We were having the time of our lives. We used to sign into Bed & Breakfast accommodation as Mr & Mrs and even bought a mock wedding band for Pauline to "legitimise" our status. Staying away from home was no longer an issue, my anxiety dissipated when I was with her. Now that our relationship was intimate, the bond between us grew stronger. I was enthralled by her beauty and very feminine ways. She was shy but had an ease, a self-assuredness about her. I, on the other hand, was awkward and self-conscious of my body, a legacy from my draconian upbringing, but it did not take me long to shake this off.

Our weekends couldn't come fast enough. We used to fill the car with all the foods we needed and took a Primus stove for cooking. Once, when we were in Kerry, we stopped at a beautiful lakeside. I thought it would be romantic to hire a small rowing boat. I didn't tell Pauline that I could barely swim and had no experience rowing. But this didn't deter me. In her company, I felt invincible and was determined to impress her. Fortunately, all went well, and we had a delightful trip around the lakes. Later that afternoon, when we were back on the road and feeling a little hungry, we decided to stop and prepare some food. The planned menu was tinned steak and kidney pie, and tinned beans, both of which needed to be heated up on the Primus.

It was a very windy day, and the flame on the Primus kept going out, so we had the brainwave to put it into the boot of the car, to shelter it from the wind. We prepared a tasty meal, but it never occurred to us that we had put a lighting Primus stove right beside the petrol tank. We could have easily been blown up in pieces and not be here to tell the tale. You don't think of these things when you're young, inexperienced and in love.

Lake in the Ring Kerry

Beach in Kerry

Both of us throwing caution to the wind!

Chapter 13

Entrepreneurial Spirit

One day I arrived at the Bon Vivant warehouse to find it was chockablock with huge boxes, and the smell of onions was overwhelming. My boss explained that he hadn't anticipated the sheer size of the two-ton consignment of dried onions he had brought in from Bulgaria. The idea was to re-pack them into small units for sale in retail stores, but he was having difficulty finding a packer to do the job at the right price. The problem now was that other new products were due to be delivered the following week and there was just no room left in the warehouse. Something had to be done and fast.

Quick on my feet, I suggested that I could set up a small packing unit and pack all the onions for £130, which was a lot of money in those days. I emphasised that I would not let this interfere with my rep's job, I would do it in my spare time, evenings and weekends. Because the Directors were under so much pressure for space, they agreed to give me a go, and I set about finding a garage to rent. Fortunately, the parents of one of my friends very generously offered me the workshop at the back of their house, free of charge. There was no shortage of staff locally to do the packing. My friends and their siblings were on school holidays and were only too delighted to be able to earn some money. And so we were ready to go!

I bought a few small battery-operated weighing scales to weigh out the required two ounces of dried onion into each small plastic pack. It wasn't long before we realised that there was no need to weigh every pack, once they were filled to the brim we had the correct amount. So we limited the weighing to the occasional spot check, which sped everything up. But the whole process was very tedious, and the smell was everywhere. We all stunk of onions, as we were covered in onion dust head to toe. You could even catch the scent on the wind as you walked up the street to the workshop.

An upside of this project was the teenage camaraderie between us. We had great fun chatting and joking among ourselves with music pumping out all day long from a transistor radio. My friend's parents allowed us access to the toilet and kitchen in their house. They also kept us supplied with refreshments and encouragement. One of my tasks was to transfer the finished products from the workshop to the company warehouse. However, we were soon facing an unforeseen issue. The product, once packed, took up much more space than the actual bulk product, and the rate at which we were packing them way exceeded the demand. So we had a buildup of stock both in the workshop and in the warehouse. The ideal solution would have been to stop packing until we had some of the finished product sold. But this was not possible as my workforce were on school holidays and were only available for a limited period. All agreed that the packing shouldn't stop and an aggressive sales campaign was put in place to drive the sales. The whole packing project took about six weeks, but it took almost two years to sell all the packs we produced.

The knowledge and practical experience I gained from this project was invaluable and would be of benefit to me in all my future business dealings. I learned that managing costs can be very challenging and time-consuming. If I didn't have the advantage and good luck of rent-free premises and cheap labour, the whole thing would have been a failure. As it was, of the £130 I received, almost £100 was profit. As for Bon Vivant, they learned that the only practical thing was to buy pre-packed products on demand. They never bought bulk dried onions again.

I had been working for Bon Vivant for about two and a half years when the company ran into financial difficulty. I was informed that they could no longer afford to keep me on, and one of the Directors would be taking up my position. They were genuinely upset about having to let me go but not half as much as I was. While I understood their difficulties, I was shocked. I had done everything that was asked of me and more. Nonetheless, my job, my company car, and my status were suddenly gone. For the first time since I was a very young boy, I found myself unemployed and without an income.

The next six months were painful. Ma complained incessantly about me being under her feet. She couldn't understand why I wasn't working, especially when there was a perfectly good, well-paid job waiting for me back at Five Star Supermarkets. I had unwisely told her when I was leaving that they said I would be welcome back if the new job didn't work out. "But that was two and a half years ago", I kept telling her. I had moved on and was only interested in a job as a Company Representative. I was prepared to wait for this and spent my days scouring the papers. While I applied for numerous jobs, every Friday, I walked three miles to Thomas Street to collect five pounds, seven shillings, and sixpence from the dole. And when I got home, Ma insisted that she get the five pounds leaving me with seven shillings and sixpence, far too little for a guy with a girlfriend. As there was no sign of a job coming, I decided to create employment for myself. I had seen how profitable the sale of ready-to-eat sausage rolls was on the delicatessen counters where I had worked. Demand was high, particularly in pubs at lunchtime, so I knew I would have no problem selling them. I bought a £60 Volkswagen car and two, second-hand cookers with my severance pay from Bon Vivant. I rented a garage in Haddington Road, secured a supply of electricity in the garage and started to make my own sausage rolls.

Early each morning, I went shopping for the ingredients. I rolled up the sausages in ready to use pastry, glazed the tops with egg yolk, and popped them in the oven. Local pubs were my main customers, and I delivered my freshly baked sausage rolls to them just before the lunchtime rush. The business was booming. I had four regular customers, and could barely keep up with the demand. However, one fateful day, in my rush to get things done, I bought skinned sausages in error. I ploughed ahead making the rolls, not knowing the plastic skins were still on. That afternoon, complaints started to pour in, ringing the death knell of my sausage roll enterprise. I would have worked to overcome the bad press and rebuild trust if it wasn't for the fact that I was barely breaking even. Once the costs of renting the premises, transportation, and raw materials were taken into account, I knew it was time to close the business. This whole experience taught me another invaluable lesson that would serve me well in the future. Even with a high-profit margin, if the actual value of your product is low, then you need to sell a lot of goods to make a significant profit.

Suffice to say, my job search was back on. I returned to combing through the papers every Sunday until, at long last, I was offered a van salesman job with Peri Crisps. I was tempted but, after some thought, decided against it, much to the annoyance of my mother. I was hellbent on getting another rep's job, with a company car. I had seen while working in supermarkets, how the van salesmen were treated very differently to sales reps, and the transition from one to the other rarely happened. It was a step back I was unwilling to take. So I continued applying for rep's jobs.

I was well-qualified for these positions and had the necessary experience under my belt. But the replies were the same every time, "Thank you for applying. We will not be proceeding with your application," or occasionally, "Sorry, the job has been filled." I didn't even get a foot in the door, let alone an interview. It began to dawn on me that giving my corporation home address might have been rendering me "undesirable." So I gave Pauline's address when applying for jobs from then on, and it worked. I got several interviews, including one for a Sales and Merchandising Representative for Beecham of Ireland. Sadly, though, the impact of social class was now crystal clear to me.

On the day of my interview, I arrived at the Beecham offices one hour early to allow plenty of time to compose myself. I even had time to drop into a local church to say a few prayers. The interview lasted an hour and a half. A week later, I was called back for a second interview and then a third and final one. I was very optimistic about this job until I received a letter in the mail a week later. The rejection wasn't new to me, but this was a big disappointment. I took some comfort in the knowledge that I had progressed so far in the interview process. And I was confident it would be just a matter of time before I secured a suitable position.

Four weeks later, I saw the same job advertised again, and I thought, *Why not? I'll give it another go.* I phoned the company to be told that they admired my bounce back, but concerning me, they had made their decision and wished me well. I was therefore surprised, about five weeks later, when I received a letter inviting me back for an interview. Filled with hope, I walked into that interview gushing confidence, assuming that after all this back and forth, if this interview went well, an offer would surely follow. However, I was back to square one, the first interview of many still ahead, but that didn't deter me.

Toward the end of the sixth interview, one of the executive's took a cigarette lighter out of his pocket, handed it to me, and asked me to sell it to him. As I began to tell him the advantages of cigarette lighters over matches, he informed me that he didn't smoke. This didn't faze me, I continued to put forward the benefits of a lighter, even to a nonsmoker. In those days, smoking was common and allowed everywhere. I thought I had it in the bag until a final comment from the sales director, Mr Skelton, set me back. "The penny hasn't dropped concerning you." To which I quickly replied, "Sometimes the penny doesn't drop immediately, but when it does, it makes a louder noise. Give me a chance, and you will hear that noise." He smiled, but I left the interview, not really knowing what the decision on me would be.

It was Wednesday, and they told me I would know by the following Friday. I waited patiently for the post that day in Pauline's house, and at eleven-thirty, the postman came by but didn't stop. That meant I was going to have to wait until Monday's post. I couldn't face the weekend without knowing, so I phoned the office to see if there was any news. Having attended so many interviews, the sales director's secretary, Nancy, knew me well. She told me the mail hadn't gone out yet, but I could expect an offer in the next few days. My heart skipped a beat. I had the job! The weekend was bliss, and this was a life-changing milestone in my life.

I started three weeks later with an induction day. Leaving the office, I had all the documentation, marketing materials, and samples I needed to do the job. Most importantly, I had the keys to my brand-new company car. On my way home, I made sure to stop by the church opposite the office to give thanks. I was quite familiar with this church by now, having called here before each of my six interviews. Whenever I am challenged about my belief in God, my reaction is the same. If in the end, he doesn't exist, then I will know I created my own protector who made it possible for me to survive and rise above my stark reality. Until that day I remain a believer.

I got home from work that day at about six o'clock and parked outside my door. It wasn't long before the neighbours were coming over to ask about my car, a beautiful white Ford Escort Estate, a rare sight, the first brand-new car on the street, and it was mine. The smell of newness was intoxicating. They all wished me well and said that I needn't worry about anybody damaging my car, they would keep an eye on it. They were even more impressed on hearing I worked at Beecham. They immediately recognised the company name from the products found in almost every house at the time: Lucozade; Brylcreem hair products; and Beecham's Pills to name but a few. I felt they were all sharing in my success and my enjoyment, and was touched by this. Landing that job at Beecham was like winning a gold medal at the Olympics, at least for me.

Ma never came out that day, but I knew she was behind the curtain, taking everything in. She should have been proud of me, just like my neighbours were. As I started unloading my samples from the car and bringing them into the house, she immediately interjected, "What are you doing? Where are you taking those? There's no room here." I looked at her in disbelief. "Ah, come on, Ma, you can't be serious?" But her face told me otherwise, and I began to panic. "What about the coal shed, can I put them there?" "No. That's my coal shed" she said. "I need that space. You'll have to find somewhere else." My mind was racing. I could feel the beads of sweat running down my temples, and my anxiety rising. What the fuck will I do now? I thought. As I started to reload the samples back into the car, Ma asked me to sit down for a moment. She stood over me and said, "Patrick, I'd like you to do something for me. First thing tomorrow morning, drive back to that company and tell them you made a mistake taking the job. Just say, thanks, but no thanks."

What she was asking me to do was outrageous. The odds against someone with my background getting a job like this were probably a million to one. And she wanted me to hand it back, without even trying. Her expectations for me were zero and took no account of my ambitions and what I dreamed of for myself. Thankfully, I had released myself from her controlling grip by then and wasn't going to allow her to destroy this magnificent hard-earned opportunity despite her efforts of sabotage. Exhausted, trying to persuade her, and once again hurt by her lack of compassion, I left the house in anger and frustration. I got into my beautiful car, drove up the hill, and started to search for a space to rent. I knocked on the doors of local private houses with garages. This was humiliating, these were my neighbours, and I was embarrassed asking for their help. After an hour and many refusals, I knocked on one last door desperately pleading my case to Mr Breen, who recognised me from my days on the horse and cart with Christy. He was very understanding and offered me a small area in his garage alongside his car. We agreed, 10 shillings a week and he gave me a key to allow me to come and go as I pleased. I was delighted with this, and as I went to leave, he casually asked why I wasn't storing my materials at home. To my surprise, I jumped to Ma's defence telling him there was just no room in my house. I wasn't going to admit to him or myself how unreasonable and vindictive she had been. She had hit at the core of my spirit, but I buried the hurt deep within and moved on.

This was my dream job, and with every week that passed, my confidence grew. The company seemed very pleased with me, and I felt I was earning my place on the sales team. We met daily for lunch in the North Star Hotel in Dublin city or in the Skylon in Drumcondra. What a treat! Not just the comradely chats and sharing of sales experiences but the lunches themselves were delicious. A whole new experience for me! Three months into my six-month probation, I was called to the office and told that they were so pleased with my performance, I could now consider myself permanent. The sales director presented me with a confirmation letter and said, "Patrick, the penny certainly has dropped." I was bursting with joy. This was my finest hour.

Some weeks later, I was called back into the office by my area manager, which in itself was not unusual. But when I got there I found the sales director, Mr Skelton, also waiting for me and both were looking very serious. I was ushered into his office and felt a little trepidation as I sat down. They cut right to the chase. "Patrick, you've been lying to us. Where do you live?" said Mr Skelton. I could feel my stomach twist into a huge knot and my mind race. I thought all was lost. So without hesitation, I faced their confrontation with bleak honesty. "If I had told the truth that I lived in a corporation house, would you have given me an interview?" There was a deafening silence. My response had taken them and me by surprise and put them on the back foot. Yes, I had lied, deserted my background to get a job. The rebel within me called it for what it was, and I was ready to take my punishment.

Then, Mr Skelton looked me in the eye, and said, "Is there anything else you've lied about?" "No" I replied, conveniently forgetting the other slight inaccuracies in my CV. I could feel myself getting upset and waffled on with heartfelt apologies. To his credit, he saw my distress and changed the subject to my sales performance. This was a welcome diversion and gave me time to compose myself. Racing through my mind was, how the hell am I going to get home without my lovely company car, and how will I explain to my family and neighbours why I had lost my job. Suddenly I heard the Sales Director say that he would let the matter go. I was shocked, this was not what I expected at all, but was delighted and very relieved. As I walked to the car, familiar feelings of embarrassment and humiliation washed over me. I buried these, as usual, and got on with it. I'm sure that when my humble background became known throughout the company, I was a talking point. But the subject was never raised in my presence. Some years later Mr Skelton asked me if I would train his son in sales. I readily agreed and put all my heart into the task, relishing the opportunity to repay, in some way, his father's kindness to me.

As my successful career at Beecham's progressed, I continued to struggle when completing my daily report sheets. My ace card was that I had Pauline there to support me. She knew about my problem and gave me a Collins pocket dictionary to help me with my spelling. It took quite a while to get used to using the dictionary. I could spend up to an hour searching for two or three words. One of my issues was that while I knew how they sounded, I got confused about the first letter. It was only through exhaustive searching through the dictionary and reading the meaning of the various words that I began to learn the spellings and memorise them. I used to carry a small notebook in which I wrote words I regularly used and could refer to. This gave me confidence and allowed me to continue covering up my problem.

Some years later while watching TV that I became aware of the condition dyslexia that would finally explain my problems with reading and writing. This came as a huge relief. But it also compounded the pain and anger that I had felt throughout my schooldays. How could the teachers not know or identify this at school? This was a condition that had been discovered more than sixty years before I was born. They could've saved me a world of harm and pain, and not just me, many others like me. Instead, I spent years where I was made to feel like I was stupid and worthless. Because of their ignorance, my curiosity and eagerness to learn were quashed. They vehemently believed I would amount to nothing and had no problem regularly telling me so. I spent all those years quietly ashamed that I hadn't learned how to properly read or write, but never openly admitting to this for fear of being crucified by one and all.

To protect myself and compensate for my dyslexia, I became street smart. At work, I diligently carried out all my duties and made sure always to be the dependable "go-to" guy. I kept my thoughts to myself, and when work and life started to come good for me, everyone but me was surprised. I learned to read people's faces and developed an incredible memory. Unfortunately, the curse of a good memory is that I can still vividly recall and relive every terrifying detail of my early years. Consequently, I had to deal with panic attacks in my twenties, and am still plagued by periodic bouts of depression.

Despite having learned to cope with dyslexia, to this day, if I am put under pressure, I still struggle to start to spell a word. Nevertheless, with the help of the treasured little dictionary that Pauline gave me, I have developed a real love of words and their meaning.

Chapter 14

Paving the Way to Happily Ever After

Pauline and I were very much in love and blissfully happy together. Marriage was clearly the next step, having been together for more than five years, and we were sure everyone would be happy for us. We went into South Anne Street in Dublin and ordered a beautiful solitaire engagement ring to be made. It was August 12, 1973, and we wanted to be sure we had it on time for Pauline's twenty-first birthday in October. It cost a lot more than we had budgeted for, but what the hell, it was worth it, and Pauline loved it. As was customary and out of respect for her parents, I called out to her home and nervously asked Pauline's Dad if I could have her hand in marriage. To our astonishment, he bluntly said, "No. You are too young to make this decision, could you not just live together for a while?" Completely shocked by this suggestion, I said, "I want to marry her, not just live with her." "We expected something better for Pauline," said Pauline's mother, out of the blue. And there it was, out in the open: I wasn't good enough for their girl. I wasn't from the right side of the tracks. Before I could reply, Pauline's Dad said to his wife, "Now, Una, that's not fair," but the words couldn't be taken back. There I was standing in Pauline's kitchen as I had frequently done and previously always felt welcome, and now I was being told I wasn't good enough. We knew nothing, and they knew everything. Our love for each other didn't seem to matter, I didn't matter, Pauline didn't matter. I was being verbally beaten up, in front of the girl I loved. My pride, my joy in what I had achieved, was all rubbished, everything belittled. This hurt me to the core, but I had taken enough abuse at home to know how to defend myself.

I began to argue my position, but the talking was going nowhere. Suddenly, Pauline's Dad blurted out, "You might be getting married, but you're not marrying Pauline." I heard him loud and clear, but nothing was going to dissuade me or make me give up the woman of my dreams. I would fight on as I had done all my life because I knew no other way. So, I turned to Pauline and asked, "Will you marry me?" and without hesitation, she said, "Yes". I had taken the risk of my life because I felt our love was strong enough to overcome anything, and it was. There was nothing more to say, so we left the house together.

Having not seen this coming, we were devastated. Tears were shed together in private as we talked about the implications. Pauline told me she couldn't understand what had just happened with her parents. She thought they had always seen her as well-grounded and intelligent. But when it came to making a decision about who to marry, they would not accept that she knew what she was doing. We decided not to announce our engagement yet, or tell my family, especially Ma. She would have been incandescent with false rage and grateful for the unsolicited help to put an end to our relationship. As far as we were concerned, our original plan to get married the following year was still firmly in place.

The engagement ring stayed in the box until Christmas Day when Pauline made the brave move to put it on and start wearing it. I was thrilled to see this and admired her courage. No one in her house remarked on the ring, clearly a sensitive issue. The silence was broken when Pauline's aunt, who came for Christmas dinner, innocently asked, "Is that an engagement ring?" and Pauline said, "Yes." Music to my ears! Her parents were not happy, but there was nothing they could do. Her mother took the approach to ignore her and our decision, for several months to come and the wedding remained unmentioned.

Shortly after Christmas, Pauline told me she could not put up with the situation at home any longer and was going to move out and find a flat near her work. While this would have been great in so many ways, I convinced her that she should stay at home and get married from her own house. We would be living together in September anyway. By Easter of 1974, it was time to finally set the date and secure a hotel for the wedding reception. When I called out to collect Pauline one day, she told me that she had decided to confront her parents. Without any preamble, I heard her say to them, "We are going out to the hotel to book the wedding reception, and I need to know if I should count you in the numbers." They were stunned, and the mood changed instantly. "Of course we'll be coming to your wedding, and I'll be paying for it" Pauline's Dad announced with pride. Her mother smiled, and the air of gloom lifted. I had steeled myself for another rejection but was pleasantly surprised with this sudden turnaround. I can only assume they were relieved that the standoff with their Pauline had come to an end—nobody had been happy about it.

From then on, her whole family engaged enthusiastically in the wedding preparations. We were giddy with excitement and anticipation. Some years later, Pauline's mother apologised for what she had said. I knew how difficult it was for her to do this, and it meant a lot to me. We became good friends over the years, but it still hurts when I think back. It had been a hard six months. I had been tested yet again, but this time I had Pauline by my side.

She had maintained a dignified silence until it was time to speak up and then, her strength and courage shone through. She made her point with an economy of words that left no one in any doubt that her mind was made up.

It was now time to deliver the good news to my family. In my naivety, I was excited about telling them, thinking that they would be happy for me. When Pauline and I called into Home Villas to share the news, Ma's initial reaction was silence. Then, showing no emotion, she took a wooden spoon from the cutlery drawer and led Pauline out into the back yard saying "Come with me, I want to show you something." I remained inside, only to be transfixed by her next move. She put the wooden spoon into a bucket of dirty socks and raised the dripping socks into the air. Although I was out of earshot, I could see what she was doing, and I was mortified. My mind reluctantly flashed back to those terrifying times when she purposefully robbed me of my dignity in the cruellest of ways. At eight, begging her on my knees not to lock me out; at ten, imploring her to help me get the teacher to stop brutalising me; at seventeen forcing me to steal for her; at twenty-one trying to sabotage my life-changing opportunity at Beecham, and now at twenty-four the ultimate humiliation and betrayal. By the time they came back into the house, panic had engulfed me. I stared at my mother with fury in my eyes, no words could convey my hurt, and after an awkward silence, we left the house.

When Pauline later told me that as Ma raised the dripping socks into the air, she had said, "Do you realise what you are marrying?", I was distraught. *What was Ma thinking? Why was she prepared to sink to the lowest level to try and prevent me from getting married? Was it greed? Was it the loss of income from me, putting her needs before mine yet again?* I wanted to turn the car around to go back and confront her. But Pauline persuaded me against it. "There is nothing more to be gained," she explained, "Your mother knows she went too far, she will have clearly seen from my reaction that her attempt to degrade you was futile."

I drove home that evening and sat outside the house in the dark. The stark reality of what I had endured over the years hit me hard. I had been conditioned by Ma into thinking this house was the only place I would be "safe," but it was the opposite. It was time, to be honest with myself and face the fact that it was a cruel home. All the imaginary magic I had attached to Ma and this house, as part of my survival strategy, was gone. I had blinded myself to her ways and, as I broke loose, the picture was clear. Having been intimidated and practically enslaved, I had become dependent on her. She would never know how much she hurt me that day of all days, but her plan had backfired. It was time for me to take control of my life. While confident in my decision, it was nonetheless a traumatic one. I had loved Ma unconditionally, to my detriment. She had purposely denied me a mother's love and protection, setting me up for a life of anxiety. To this day, I avoid allowing her into my thoughts. I believe there is a narrow line between sanity and madness. And that, on many occasions, I came perilously close to that line, because of her cruelty. When thinking back, I am careful not to dwell too long on what I endured for fear that I might cross that line and lose control of my sanity. That part of my heart that was her's and her's alone remains broken.

As my wedding day got closer, Ma gave me the silent treatment but tolerated me as long as she got her money every week. This included an additional two shillings for each shirt she washed and ironed for me. I welcomed the distance between us and, came and went as I pleased. There were no chats about my upcoming wedding, no sense of happiness or excitement. However, when the wedding invitations went out, all my family accepted - keeping up appearances was paramount in our family. I even asked Ken to be my best man, believing as my older brother, this was his right. He accepted without hesitation and couldn't have been more helpful. So much so, that I wondered if I had been unfair in my prior judgement of him. Unfortunately, after a few months, he reverted to form, and I knew I hadn't been wrong.

None the less, he was a great help around the time of the wedding and helped make it a joyous occasion.

One day Philomena, Da, and myself were in the kitchen, and Philomena asked what I was giving Pauline as the customary silver token on our wedding day. Immediately, my Da got up from his seat saying "Just wait a moment" and left the room. He appeared back with a brand new shiny US dollar which he handed to me saying "This is from a special mint and should be worth a lot in the future". I cherished this for years, believing he had given me something special, passing on something important to him, father to son. A few years after he died, I was disappointed to learn from a coin expert that it was silver coated and only worth its face value. Da also raised the issue of our honeymoon that day. He recommended Malta, where he had been for the past few years on his annual holiday. He raved about the beauty of the place, the palatial hotels and the added bonus, English was the spoken language. In those days there was no direct flight to Malta so a connection in Rome would be required and Da offered to gift us all the flight tickets. His sudden generosity was out of character but most welcome. I was delighted and proud of my Da that day. Meanwhile, we had found a lovely studio flat in Malahide. This was a well-to-do seaside village on the Northside of Dublin and ideally located for both our jobs.

On the morning of my wedding, I woke early and, as I put my feet to the cold floor, I was aware of something surreal happening to me. My senses were heightened, and as I stood up, I noticed, for the first time, how small the room was. My eye was drawn to the plastic bag in the corner. This contained the sum total of my belonging and my life in this house. I opened the bedroom door to the tiny upstairs landing and was reminded of the times when, Philomena and I knelt there, as kids, in our nightwear. We only dared to do this when there were visitors, and we could listen in on the goings-on downstairs while Ma was distracted entertaining. As I came down the steep, narrow stairs, I thought to myself, *why has it taken me until this, my last day here, to notice how small and insignificant life was in this house?* And there was the answer to my question, it was my last day here. Somehow, it felt as though I was reliving all my experiences of this place and the people I shared it with. And their power to intimidate me faded away in front of my eyes, revealing their true nature. While I would usually be ebullient on entering the kitchen, on this occasion, I didn't feel the need to even initiate a conversation. I felt totally liberated.

There was no excitement in the house, nothing special other than it being the most important day of my life. There were no words of advice or kindness, just the nothingness, which I had sadly grown to expect. Thankfully Pauline's brother Paddy stopped by to bring me for a hair cut at his favourite barbershop off Grafton Street. This was so unlike the local one in Donnybrook, which I had frequented since a child. Until I was tall enough, the barber would sit me up on a piece of wood laid across the arms of the adult chair. Every time I went, I asked him to try and avoid slicing off the small skin tag on my scalp, but he always managed to draw blood. I can still feel that sharp pain when he applied the antiseptic lotion to stop the bleeding. Now that I had experienced how pain-free a haircut could be, I would never go back to the old barber's shop again.

My two brothers travelled with me in a black limousine to the church where most of my family were waiting. They were all in great form. Despite living only two minutes away, Pauline was running late. But I was quite relaxed taking in the atmosphere until the moment arrived and she was there. When the church doors opened, I saw what I can only describe as a vision of beauty, on her father's arm. There was a halo of sunlight wrapped around her stunning silhouette. And as she took the final steps towards me and slipped her hand in mine, I thought to myself, *I'm not alone anymore.*

Within thirty minutes we were husband and wife and on our way to celebrate this momentous occasion in a hotel in Bray, County Wicklow. A slight detour brought us to the Dominican Convent in Donnybrook where Pauline had been educated, and

Pauline and her Dad arriving at the
Church of the Assumption Booterstown. 1974

Husband and Wife at last

Signing the Past Pupils' Register at
Muckross Park Convent Donnybrook

we signed the Past Pupils' Register. I, unlike Pauline, had no happy memories to acknowledge and had no inclination to revisit my 'alma mater' that day. I'm sure they were shattered!

Once we got to the hotel, we sat down for a candlelight dinner, and after the speeches, my Ma and Da came to say their goodbyes. It was quite unusual for the parents of the groom to leave so early. I suppose they were reluctant attendees anyway so I shouldn't have been too surprised, but I was disappointed. We danced the rest of the night away to a live band. Fantastic! This was the best day of my life. I could not have been happier.

The following day, we headed off to Rome and checked into the Hotel Richmond. This was a small boutique hotel opposite the Colosseum. We hadn't a word of Italian, but this only became an issue when we were choosing from the menu at local Italian restaurants. Then it was a total guessing game. We were served some very attractive-looking dishes, none of which were to our liking. But this was all part of the adventure of our first continental holiday together. Our most memorable meal in Rome was a takeaway roast chicken, some fresh Italian bread, and a family-sized bottle of Coke. We devoured these sitting on our hotel bed with the windows wide open to the magnificent view and the sound of cars beeping incessantly below, as they circled the Colosseum. Chicken never tasted so good! This was one of those extra special memories that stay with you forever.

Malta was everything we expected. Our hotel was luxurious, overlooking Julian's Bay with its beautiful azure blue water, and the sun shone every day we were there. Since everything was inexpensive, we didn't give money a second thought until we returned to Rome and discovered we were running short. We had no credit cards then, so Ken wired fifty pounds to the Irish Embassy to keep us going during what remained of our honeymoon.

By our last day we were broke again and ready to go home, but we still had one more unforeseen hurdle to cross. When we got to the airport, we found that there was a problem with our flight tickets home. I explained to the girl at the ticket desk that my father, who worked at Dublin airport, had given them to us as a wedding gift. She looked up at us sympathetically and said in broken English, "Unfortunately, these are standby tickets. You can use these if there are spare seats, and there aren't any today, the plane is full." I was dumbfounded. There was a slight possibility that some of the passengers booked for that flight might not show, but, we would have to wait until the last minute for confirmation.

I could not believe what Da had done. As an airport staff member, he could have bought discounted tickets. But he chose standby tickets instead, the cheapest possible option, knowing full well the risks that came with this. He had gambled that everything would go smoothly, and no one would be the wiser. He took the gamble, and we were paying the price. Worst of all, he hadn't explained any of this to us, so here we were stranded at Rome's airport with no flight home. As we sat there, not knowing what to do, luck was on our side. Just as we had resigned ourselves to staying at the airport all night, we heard our names being called. Two seats had become available, but we might have to surrender them at a Lourdes stopover if needed. The flight was about to take off, so we ran what seemed like a mile dragging our cases behind us. We were in a right panic by the time we got to the plane. When we landed at Lourdes, our fingers were crossed that we wouldn't be asked to get off. I then saw my ex-girlfriend's father and sister come on the plane and all I could think of was everyone in Donnybrook would hear Pat Lee and his bride were put off the plane. Just then I saw the doors being closed and I breathed a sigh of relief. We were safe and on our way home, no thanks to my Dad. I had been so impressed with such a fantastic wedding gift, and for the life of me, I can't understand why he short-changed us. He was now hurting Pauline, and this is where I drew the line. I would never again expect anything from him, we were done.

When we arrived at Dublin Airport, Ken and Pauline's mother were waiting there to bring us to her house for a meal and catch up. We had to pass by Home Villas on the way, but there was no question of us dropping in. Without an invitation, we would not be welcome. Everyone was delighted to see us at

Booterstown. And after a sumptuous meal, "Manna from heaven," we reminisced about the wedding and shared some of our honeymoon adventures, never once mentioning the difficulties we had at the airport coming home. At the end of the evening, we said our goodbyes and headed over to our new home. This was the perfect romantic hideaway. The annexe to a large house, it had its own front door, a parking space, and a private patio area at the back. It was delightful.

Now that we were living together, I felt free for the first time. What was impossible before became possible. There were no restrictions on me. I no longer had to ask permission to turn on the TV or to take a bath. I could eat whenever I wanted and had ample wardrobe space. But more than anything, I was with the girl I loved. Our flat was just a short walk to the quaint village and a long sandy beach. At the weekends, we went for long walks along the strand, and to our favourite coffee shop nearby. At the delicatessen store in the village, we stocked up on fresh bread and delicious foods. We always ate by candlelight in our cosy den and those long nights during our first winter living together were magical. Our large comfy bed, in the centre of the main living area, was piled high with soft rugs and fluffy pillows. This was our favourite spot to sit and watch television, listen to music, and chat for hours planning and dreaming about our future.

Our life was bliss. We were together, and nothing could diminish our happiness. We were finally living our dreams, true to the words of the "Seekers" song we sang at our wedding reception:

We'll build a world of our own

That no one else can share

All our sorrows we'll leave

Far behind us there

And I know you will find

There'll be peace of mind

When we live in a world of our own.

Feedback welcome
to
patrickmlee@hotmail.co.uk

Leaving our Wedding Reception to start our life together

CPSIA information can be obtained
at www.ICGtesting.com
Printed in the USA
LVHW081941111221
705928LV00010BA/37